Sweet Dreams
Heirloom Quilts for Babies

Deborah Gordon

&

Helen Frost

To our babies -
Matthew and Christopher
&
Sarah, Rebecca, Paul and Rachel

ACKNOWLEDGEMENTS

Our heartfelt thanks to Kathy Blair and Nancy Thompson for helping with the photography and to Pam Mauss and Suzanne Elliott for lending us their baby items. A special thank you to Betty Alderman for the wonderful scissor-cuttings.

Illustrations by the authors

Photography by Chuck Rausin
La Habra, California

Cover photograph by Jack Mathieson
Woodland Hills, California

Typesetting by Wendy Voorhees
Tucson, Arizona

Printed by Arizona Lithographers
Tucson, Arizona

Published by First Star
10237 East Rio de Oro
Tucson, Arizona
(520) 885-7278

© Copyright 1995 by Helen Frost and Deborah Gordon

All rights reserved. No part of this work covered by the copyright hereon may be reproduced or used in any form or by any means without written permission of the publisher.

ISBN: 0-9633917-3-9

Contents

Introduction · 5
Materials · 7
Piecing Techniques · 10
Appliqué Techniques · 17
Finishing Techniques · 21
Rockabye Baby · 28
Ring Around the Rosey · 30
Night and Noon · 41
Baby Blocks · 43
Good Morning, Sunshine! · 44
Dancing Fans · 46
Pat-a-Cake · 48
Daisy Chain · 50
Little Gosling Chase · 52
Sweet Hearts · 54
Ribbon Twist · 56
Twinkle, Twinkle · 58
Bright Hopes · 60
Duck and Ducklings · 62
Baby Bunting · 64
Whiligig · 66
Railroad Crossing · 68

Introduction

Sleep, baby, sleep
Thy father guards the sheep
Thy mother shakes the dreamland tree
And from it fall sweet dreams for thee
Sleep, baby, sleep

A mother wishes for sweet dreams as her baby slumbers peacefully, wrapped in a soft, pretty quilt. This special quilt, made with loving hands, was a gift – a gift just for being born.

We believe the miracle of birth deserves the finest of needlework – wonderful designs, intricate piecing, elegant appliqué and lots of quilting. The quilts presented here were made as heirlooms, meant to be used graciously and kept for future generations to treasure. Some of the patterns are simple and can be easily pieced in an afternoon. With hand quilting and an interesting finish these quilts will be just as special as the more complex designs.

Since many baby quilts are also their makers' first quilt, we have been very thorough in all our directions. Through text and illustrations, we're there to guide you every step of the way. If you're a more experienced quilter, you still will find a different method or new technique or two.

Most crib sized quilts measure about 45 by 54 inches. As mothers, we know that quilts are also used in cradles, bassinets, strollers, car seats, over shoulders, and of course, to wrap around a baby. For this reason, we have included a variety of sizes. Most can easily be made smaller or larger, if you prefer a different size.

We realize that we are rather opinionated about the best way to make quilts (almost as definite as we are in our ideas on raising children)! Although we give lots of advice on every aspect of making quilts, we realize that all a baby really needs or wants is a cover that is soft and warm. With that in mind, we wish you success with your quilt and hope that it is soft as a baby's breath and as warm as a mother's love.

Materials

This collection of quilts was designed with all quilters in mind, the novice as well as the accomplished. For that reason, we have included quilts that only require a few fabrics as well as some that use many. The beginner will find a planned color scheme simpler to do; the experienced quilter will appreciate using some of her fabric collection in a scrap-type quilt.

FABRICS

Good quality, muslin weight, woven fabrics in 100% cotton are best suited for patchwork and quilting. Cotton is the best for patchwork and a must for appliqué since it holds a crease better and is less likely to fray.

Although knits are ideal for baby clothes, they are unsuitable for piecing and appliqué. The same is true of flannel; the soft texture is inviting, but flannel frays and will not hold together because of the small seams used in patchwork. Also, many of the so-called flannels are actually brushed synthetics and of poor quality.

Prints and Patterns

Choosing the fabrics is one of the most enjoyable parts of making a quilt and it's even more fun with a baby quilt. There are so many wonderful prints made today that the entire room can be coordinated around the showpiece quilt. Nursery prints, with such classic motifs as baby toys or characters from Mother Goose rhymes, are not necessary in a baby quilt, but will certainly add charm.

Since all of the blocks presented here are sized relatively small – in keeping with the small size of the quilts – the prints used should be smaller in scale. We have used some splashy florals, but the flowers still only measure one or two inches. Make a window template to see if the scale of the print is in proportion to the scale of the quilt block. Draw the pattern piece without seams on card stock and cut out the shape with sharp scissors or a craft knife. Place the window template on the fabric to see how it will look pieced in the quilt.

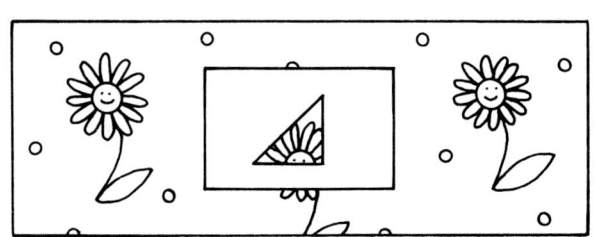

The multi-fabric quilts should include a good mix of patterns, such as dotted, geometrical, abstract, and floral. If all florals are preferred, try to vary the size and density of the flowers.

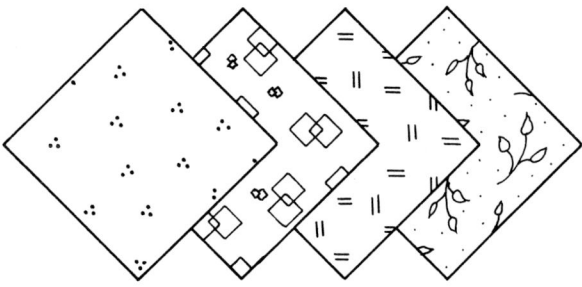

Traditionally, a variety of prints are combined with a solid background. If decorative quilting is planned for the background areas, it is better to use a plain or a tiny print so the quilting will show to an advantage. Another approach combines a multi-colored background with solids, or solid-appearing prints, in the colors found in the background print.

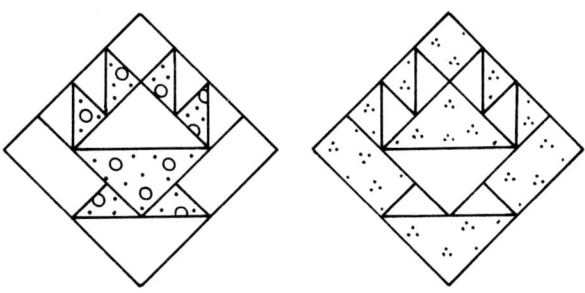

Color
Many things will determine the color scheme for the quilt. The new mother probably has already selected specific colors for the baby's room. If the child hasn't arrived, you might want to use peach instead of pink, just in case it's a boy. For an older child, you may want to use richer or deeper colors rather than the pastels usually reserved for newborns. We have included a wide range of possible color schemes in our quilts. Let the photographs spark ideas and possible schemes.

Colors vary in their clarity. Many of the fabrics available today are grayed or muted, meaning that gray has been added to the color. A clear color has very little added gray. If both clear and grayed colors are used in the same quilt, the grayed fabric may look dirty or dingy compared to the clear color.

The color value of the fabrics should also be considered. Value is the lightness or darkness of a color, or its visual weight. Value is also relative. A medium value fabric will appear light when placed next to a dark fabric. That same color will appear dark when place with a very light fabric. The use of medium value fabrics, since they can be used as both light and dark, increases the visual interest in a quilt.

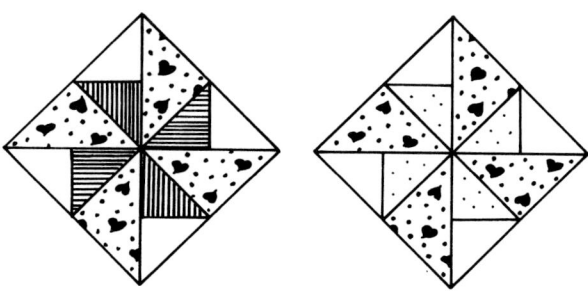

Occasionally, a quilt has a fabric that is too light to have been used with a particular background fabric. The fabric does not show well against the background and the piece drops out or disappears from the design. Always view the fabric combinations from a distance of about ten feet. Since a quilt is worked on so closely, it's easy to forget that the finished product will also be seen from a distance.

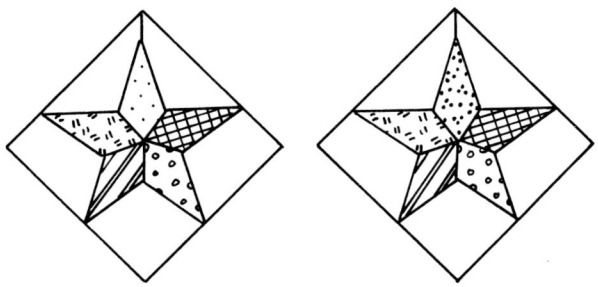

Design Variations
Be sure to consider any possible design variations as you make the quilt. We offer many different sizes and types of quilts, but you can still personalize the quilts further. Be creative! Be inspired by your fabrics and modify the design to suit your needs and wants.

Remember that the yardage requirements are for the quilts as shown. To use fewer fabrics than specified, add the various amounts. To make a scrappier quilt, divide the yardage amounts by the number of fabrics to be used, allowing some extra for each.

The yardage amounts are based on a usable width of 42 inches. The fabric amounts allow for a few extra inches, both for shrinkage and mistakes! Many of the pieces will not use the whole width of the fabric, so smaller scraps from your own collection may be substituted. The quilt directions refer to our color choices; cut swatches of your own fabrics to make following the directions easier.

Fabric Preparation
All fabrics should be preshrunk before using. This removes excess sizing, dye, and processing chemicals, as well as allowing the fabric to shrink before it is sewn into the quilt. Wash or rinse the fabrics in a washing machine, or soak them in a sink full of warm water. Do not wash more than six yards of fabric at one time because it will wrinkle.

After the fabrics are dried, they should be pressed. Since washing removes the sizing, use a little spray starch or sizing to add body to the fabric. This also makes it easier to mark and cut the quilt pieces.

BATTING

Consider the probable use when choosing a batting. A small quilt that will mainly be used as a wrap or bunting should have light weight batting. A quilt hung on the wall as decoration will look better with a flatter, more traditional batt. A slightly thicker, fluffier batting will work well for use in a crib or playpen. Try not to choose a batting on its appearance or feel, since it will be completely encased in the quilt. Instead, wrap a piece of fabric around a layer of the batting to test the weight and feel. Do a few test stitches through the layers, testing the thickness.

Polyester battings are available in several different weights and types. This light, fluffy batting needles very easily and since it does not migrate (pull apart and form lumps), the lines of quilting can be as far as four inches apart. Polyester makes a very warm cover since it does not breathe as natural fibers do.

Cotton batting gives the quilt a flatter profile, similar to antique quilts. Unless closely quilted, the batting will shift when the quilt is washed. A cotton/polyester blend batting also gives the flatter profile but can be quilted further apart.

Wool batting will give a traditional look and feel to the quilt. Although wool is heavier in feel it still needles very easily. Wool resists migration because of the configuration of the fibers but still should be closely quilted. This batting can cause problems if there are wool allergies and is more expensive than other battings. Follow the manufacturers directions when laundering the quilt.

Batting should be taken from the package a few days before using to allow the folds and creases to relax. Putting it in a dryer for a few minutes on the permanent press cycle will also help it fluff.

Piecing Techniques

Whether the sewing is by hand or machine, the joining of the many geometric shapes in a patchwork quilt is called piecing. Some patterns are ideal for machine work; others can be made better and sometimes easier by hand.

Templates
Templates can be made from several materials, such as plastic or lightweight cardboard. We prefer the plastic that is made specifically for templates since the edges will not change shape with use. Sheets of acetate are too brittle and will be difficult to cut.

Trace the pattern, using the line that is correct for the sewing technique, and transfer all the marks such as grainline arrows. Trace very carefully, using a ruler for straight lines. Trace curved shapes by making dots along the line. This is more accurate than trying to follow the curve. Cut the templates, again being very careful and accurate. Label the templates with the size and name of the block, the letter of the piece, and whether the template includes the seam allowance.

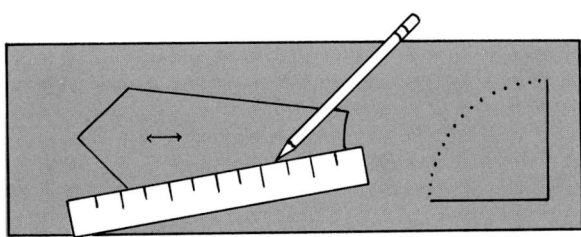

Most of the pattern pieces have been drafted with squared corners on the seam allowances. This aids in placing the pieces and makes the sewing and matching easier.

The grainline of each piece is an important factor in the success of the finished quilt. Since the lengthwise grain has no stretch, and the crosswise very little, the outside edges of the pieces are placed on these grainlines. If special effects are desired, such as a printed motif centered in a square, or a stripe cut in a certain direction, the grainline arrows will have to be ignored. However, these pieces will require very careful handling.

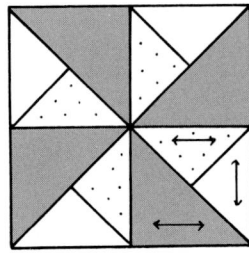 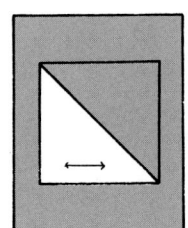 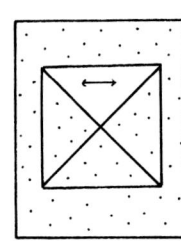

Marking
Always mark and cut the larger pieces first, including any strips for the borders. We prefer not to have a seam in our borders so we have allowed for most of

the borders to be cut on the lengthwise grain of the fabric. Only on borders measuring less than 42 inches do we cut on the crosswise grain. Use the excess fabric for the smaller pieces.

Begin marking on the bottom edge of the fabric and work upward. This keeps the excess fabric on the table instead of your lap. Place the templates with the grainline arrows parallel to the lengthwise or crosswise grain of the piece. A piece of double-stick tape will help hold the template in place.

Place the templates on the wrong side of the fabric. The lines will show better on the wrong side and any sewing lines need to be on that side. Mark around the template, using a pencil on light colored fabrics or a chalk pencil on dark fabrics. A dull point makes a wider line and changes the shape of the pattern. We like mechanical pencils for their consistently fine lines. Use a soft lead for easy marking.

Some patterns require mirror images of the template. This is noted on the pattern piece and in the directions with a small "r" following the letter of the pattern piece, such as "A" and "Ar." Turn the template face down, or cut the fabric folded, to yield the reverse shape.

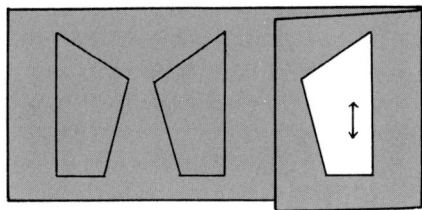

Cutting
Good, sharp fabric scissors or shears are used to cut several layers of fabric at a time. Cut only as many layers as can be done accurately. The layers can be several different fabrics, or just one folded or layered on itself. The fabric should be folded right sides together only if the templates are symmetrical. Scissors should be held straight, since angling to either side will make the bottom pieces a different size.

The rotary cutter and mat can be used in cutting some of the pieces. They are great for cutting strips, borders, and bindings. We have included rotary cutting measurements on the templates whenever suitable. The fabric should be squared before any pieces or strips are cut. Great care should be taken that the ruler is always placed perpendicular to the folds of the fabric. This insures straight strips, instead of angled ones.

We have included the sizes of some of the larger pieces. Cut as directed, then cut again, with scissors or rotary cutter, to make the needed shape.

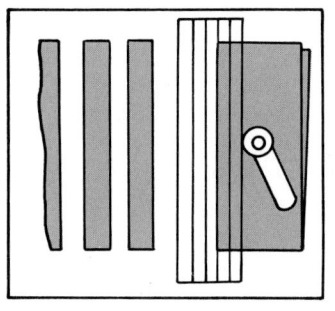 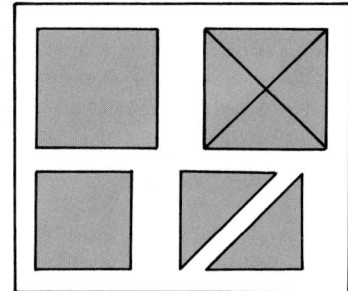

HAND PIECING TECHNIQUES

Hand sewing was the only method available to quilters two centuries ago and is still the preferred method of many of today's quilters. It is very portable, and can be done almost anywhere. The rhythmic stitching is similar to quilting, but since the stitches do not show, it is even more relaxing. Most of all, hand piecing is very precise. Some patterns, such as those with curves or angles, are actually easier to piece by hand. The joining of the finished blocks can be done on the machine.

Cutting
The templates are made without the outer cutting line, so the line marked on the fabric is the sewing line. Mark on the wrong side of the fabric, and place the shapes at least ½ inch apart, to allow for the seams. Cut ¼ inch away from the marked lines.

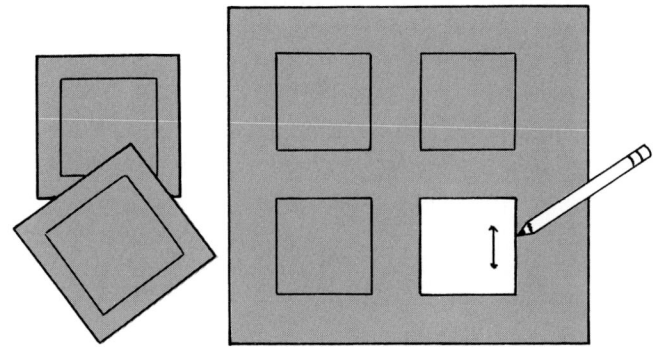

It's easier to use two sets of templates, with and without the seam allowance. The template with the seams is used to mark the cutting line on one or more layers, then the template without the seams is used to mark the sewing line.

If many pieces from the same template are needed, it is better to cut layers. Fold the fabric (if the templates are symmetrical) and pin the layers before cutting. Cut only as many layers as can be done accurately.

Sewing

Use a fine needle, either a betweens in sizes 10 or 12 or a sharps in size 10 or 11. Thread the needle with about 18 inches of sewing or quilting thread. Tie a beginning knot. Pin two pieces of the block together at the ends of the sewing lines, and in between if necessary. Match the lines while pinning. Begin sewing at the first pin, taking small, even running stitches. This is done by pushing the needle with one thumb and index finger, and at the time, manipulating the fabric in a subtle up and down motion with the other hand. Take several stitches before pulling the needle through, turning the piece over to verify that the stitching is on both marked lines. End the stitching at the corner, making an ending knot. Finger press each seam, or lightly press with a dry iron.

As the block is assembled, the stitching should not cross a previously sewn seam. Sew up to the seam, anchor the stitching with a backstitch, then pass the needle through the base of the opposing seams. Move the seams away from the needle and continue stitching on the other side. The seam allowances will remain flexible.

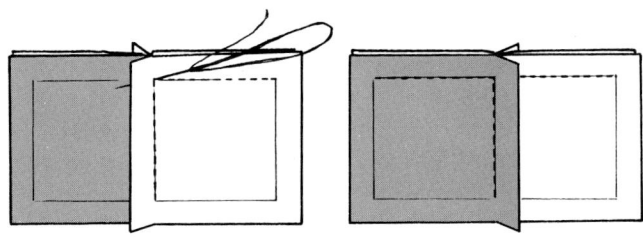

This technique makes setting in angled pieces very easy. Pin and sew only one side of the set-in piece at a time. Pass through, rather than sew over, the opposing seam. Then pivot the piece and continue sewing the other side.

Making Beginning Knots

Method 1 – Hold the end of the thread between thumb and forefinger. Wrap the thread once over the finger, crossing the end of the thread. Bring the needle under the thread and out, forming a single knot for piecing, appliqué or quilting.

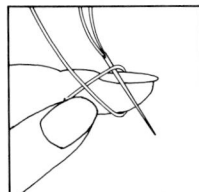 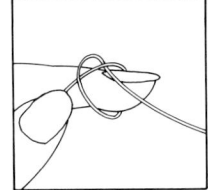 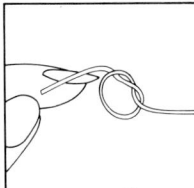

Method 2 – Hold the end of the thread so it faces the tip of the needle. Place the end of the thread between the two fingers holding the needle. Wrap the thread around the needle two or three times. Cover the wraps with the fingers that held the needle and pull the needle with the the other hand. Slide the wraps to the end of the thread where they become a knot. Use fewer wraps for a small knot for quilting and more for a larger knot for piecing or appliqué.

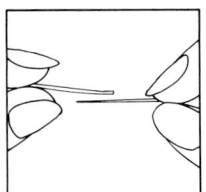 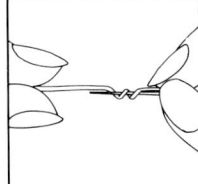 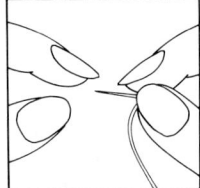

Making Ending Knots

Method 1 – Complete the line of stitching, then make another stitch next to the last one to anchor the needle. Bring the single thread from the last stitch across the needle and behind it. Leaving the loop of thread below the eye, bring the double thread alongside the needle. Cross the other thread and bring the double threads behind the needle. Pull the needle out, forming a secure knot for piecing or appliqué.

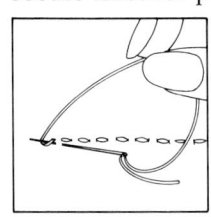 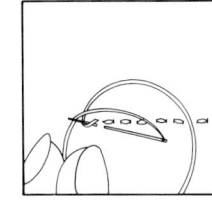 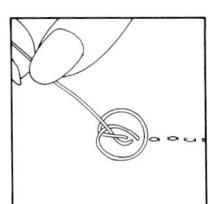

Method 2 – Complete the line of stitching, then anchor the needle with one more small stitch. Holding only the double thread coming from the eye of the needle, pass the threads behind the tip of the needle. Cross over and wrap the threads behind the eye end. Once more, cross over and wrap the threads behind the tip. Pull the needle out, forming a good knot for piecing or appliqué.

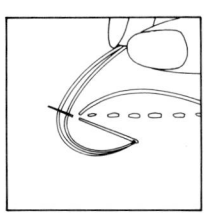 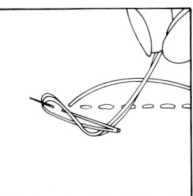 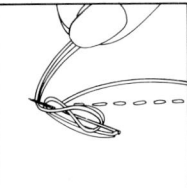

Piecing Techniques

Center Seams

Whenever several seams converge at the center, it's possible to pass through all the opposing seams. However, this will result in a tiny hole in the center. Instead, pass through one seam at a time and take a tiny stitch each time. The tiny stitches are nearly on top of each other, but they lock the center together.

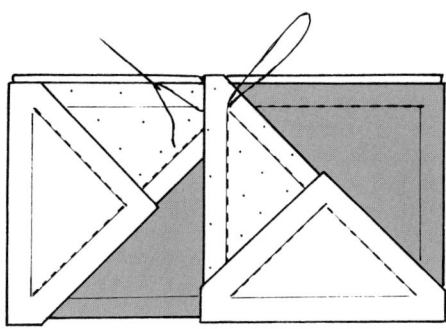

Continuous Piecing

It's also possible to do continuous piecing when sewing by hand. Each new piece is added on to the sewn pieces, without breaking the thread. The triangles in *Baby Bunting* were sewn this way, with one thread used for each arc. When a block has a center design, such as the star in *Twinkle, Twinkle,* the background pieces can be added in one continuous seam. Don't pin all the pieces together, just pin and sew one seam before adding the next piece.

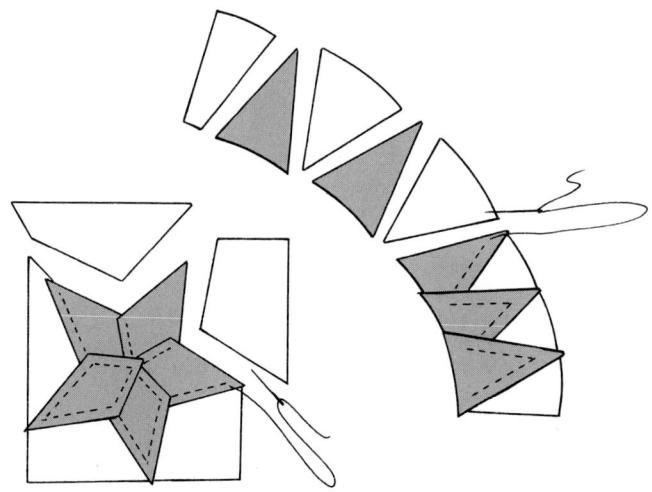

Curved Seams

Some extra care should be taken with curved seams. Be sure to transfer all the marks from the templates. It is not necessary to clip anywhere on either piece. The fullness is handled best if the concave piece is the top layer while piecing. Bending the fabric gently over a finger will help to evenly distribute the fullness. Pin at the ends and at the center mark. Pin and sew along the seam line, taking only two or three stitches at a time to ensure a smooth curved seam.

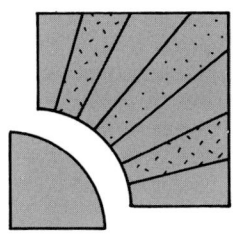 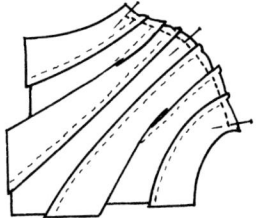

Pressing

As each block is completed, press it following the pressing diagram. In most cases, the seams are pressed away from the background fabrics. Use a dry iron since steam can distort the blocks.

PAPER PIECING

Paper piecing is a technique that improves the precision and ease of sewing certain shapes. The fabric pieces are basted over paper shapes, then joined together by hand. When the patchwork is completed, the basting stitches and papers are removed.

Make two sets of templates; with and without seam allowances. Cut pieces from white or natural colored construction paper without seams. Cut the fabric pieces with seams.

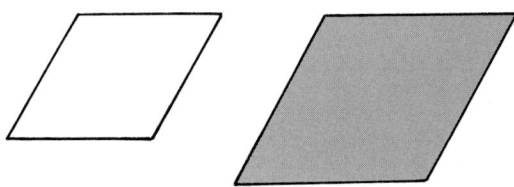

Pin a paper piece in the center of the wrong side of the fabric piece. Using a contrasting thread, baste the seam allowance in place through the paper. Make one stab stitch at a time.

After all the pieces are basted, arrange them into the design. Place two pieces right sides together, matching the folded edges. Using a single strand of sewing thread in a matching color and a betweens needle, make small whip stitches through the folds. Don't pierce the folds too deeply or the stitches will show from the front of the patchwork. As more pieces are added, it may be necessary to fold some of the shapes in half.

The pieces are joined into sections, then rows. Join the rows to complete the top. It's best to leave the papers in place until the top is finished and ready to quilt. The papers help the top retain the correct shape, but also keep the seams flat. As the basting threads are clipped and removed, the papers will simply fall out. They can be reused in another project.

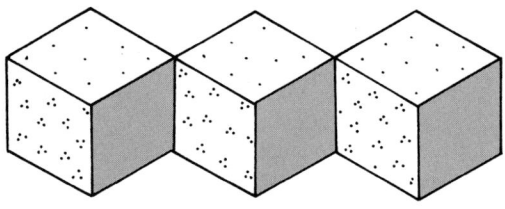

MACHINE PIECING TECHNIQUES

When the sewing machine was introduced in 1846, quilters did not waste any time in using the new device to make quilts. Quilt designs with mostly straight seams as well as any strip piecing should certainly be done on the sewing machine.

Cutting

Make the templates with the seam allowance included. Layers of fabric can be cut together since the sewing line usually does not have to be marked.

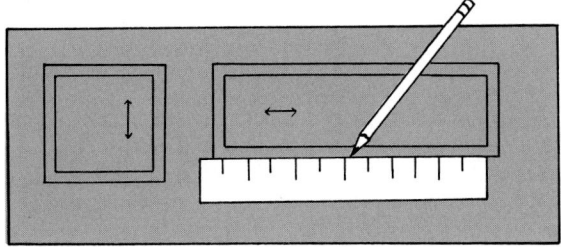

Mark on the wrong side of the fabric, since it's easier to see the marks on that side. Place the pieces with a common line whenever possible. Either press the fabrics with spray starch between the layers or pin to keep the layers from shifting. Cut only as many layers as can be done easily and accurately. Four layers is usually the best.

Sewing

It's important to establish an accurate ¼ inch seam allowance. Sew an inch or two with the machine unthreaded, then measure from the dotted line made by the needle to the edge of the pieces. This should measure a scant ¼ inch. The edge of the presser foot can be used as a guide, adjusting the needle position if necessary. Sometimes a mark or tape can be placed on the throat plate of the machine.

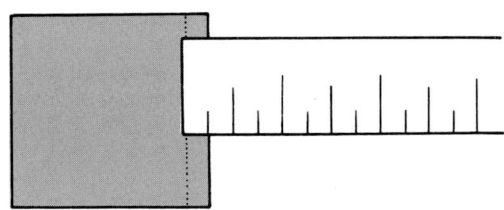

The quilt directions each include a block assembly diagram. In each, the smallest units are sewn first, then added to the larger pieces. Always try to begin a seam at the blunt ends of the pieces since most machines have the tendency to catch pointed pieces in the throat plate hole. Sew from edge to edge, not just on the sewing line. When sewing a straight grain piece to a bias edge piece, place the bias on the bottom. This takes advantage of the sewing machine's tendency to stretch the top layer and ease the bottom layer.

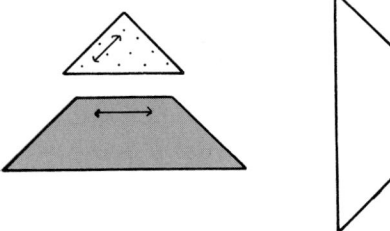

Thread the machine with regular sewing thread in a light neutral color. Use a fine needle (size 11 or 70) and sew with about twelve stitches to the inch. It is not necessary to backstitch.

Instead of ending the thread after each piece, continue on to the next. Either chain piece the different parts of one block or chain piece the same parts of all the blocks, assembly-line style. Watch for mirror-image placement while chain piecing. Sew half the pieces with one fabric on top, then sew the other half with the other fabric on top.

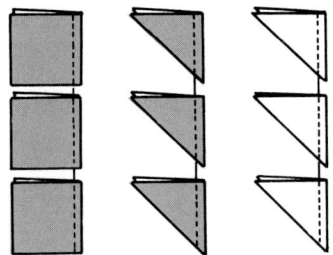

Leave the various units connected until they are pressed. Press a whole string of triangles or squares, then clip the threads. This saves time and handling. It's also easy to press only from the front. Place the fabric that the seam will be pressed toward on top. Use the iron to open the piece as it is pressed.

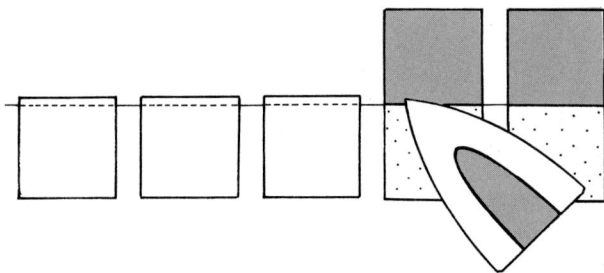

Matching Seams
Place the seams in opposite directions for a perfect match. Pin, perpendicular to the stitching line, to keep the layers from shifting. Sew slowly over each seam junction, taking the pin out before the needle reaches it. Make sure the seam allowance on the bottom does not flip in the wrong direction.

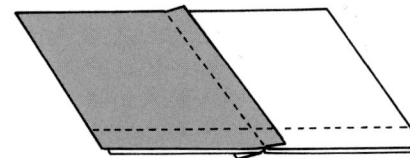

When several points must match at the seam, place the pin where the points converge. There may not be a full ¼ inch seam on both layers but it's more important for the points to match. Any part of the block that is hard to match, such as center seams or points, can be machine basted first. Sew that area with a very long stitch, check to see if it matches, then sew again with a smaller stitch.

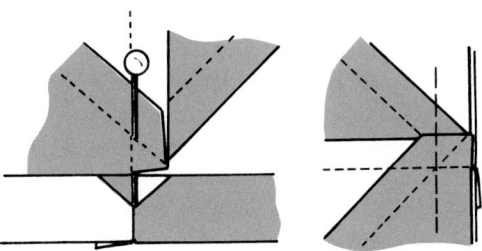

Angled Seams
Angles can be sewn by machine by stopping the stitching on the sewing line. Pin and sew only one side of the angled piece at a time, stopping at the center seam and backstitching one stitch. Lift the needle and presser foot and move the center seam away from the line of stitching. Insert the needle, and pivot the piece. Lower the presser foot, stitch in place to secure the threads, then continue sewing.

An angled seam can also be sewn in two steps. Keeping the corner seam allowance free, sew on side of the piece, then the other. Begin and end each seam with backstitching.

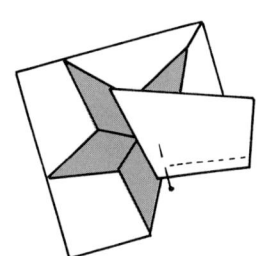 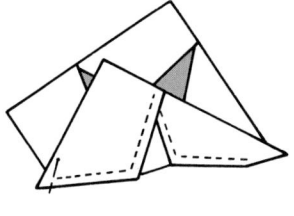

Curved Seams
Even curves can be sewn on the machine with careful and frequent pinning. It's also important to have the convex piece on the bottom, to take advantage of the sewing machine's tendency to ease in the bottom layer. It is not necessary to clip either piece. Sew slowly, making sure tiny pleats are not sewn into the seam.

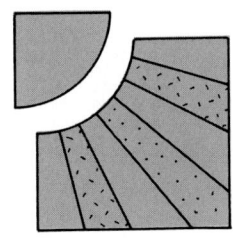 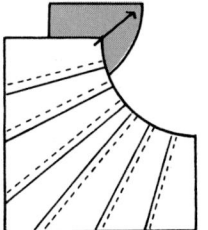

Strip Piecing

Some of the designs utilize the method of strip piecing. Strips are cut and sewn together, then cut again into sections. Cut the strips as directed, using scissors or the rotary cutter, and sew with ¼ inch seams. Chain piece the strips in groups. Press the strips, then mark and cut into the specified sections. These sections are then sewn into the various blocks.

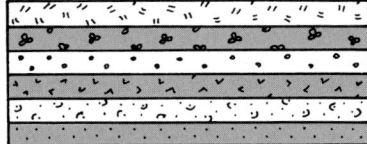 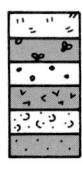 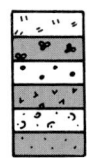

Grid Triangle Piecing

Triangles are sometimes difficult to piece accurately because the machine may stretch and distort the bias edges, or catch the tips in the throat plate. An innovative method prevents these problems by sewing the diagonal seam on right-angle triangles before they are cut.

Mark a grid of squares on the wrong side of the lighter colored of the two fabrics. The size of the square is the finished measurement of the short side of the triangle plus ⅞ inch. Mark one square for every two triangles needed. Make diagonal lines in alternating directions through each square, as shown.

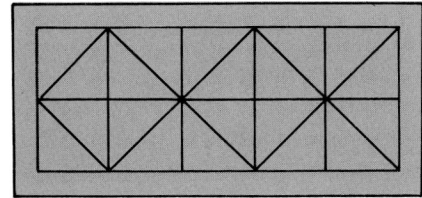

Cut around the grid, leaving an inch of excess fabric. Cut the same size piece from the other fabric. Place the two layers right sides together and pin. Sew ¼ inch from the diagonal lines. Mark the seam lines if necessary, since any guides on the machine will be covered by the fabric. After cutting the squares apart, cut on the diagonal lines, between the two lines of stitching. Press the seams toward the darker fabric. These triangle-squares are joined with the other pieces to make the block.

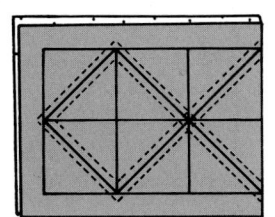 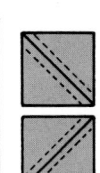  

Assembling the Blocks

Press the sections of each block before assembling them. It's always a good idea to square the sections of a block before they are joined. If triangles look too pointed or the edges of pieces are uneven, measure and trim as needed.

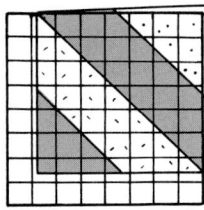 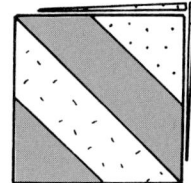

The sections of the blocks can be chain pieced. Sew the sections in order and leave them connected. The threads will keep the top and bottom halves in position for the next seam.

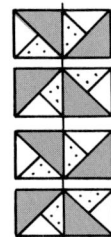 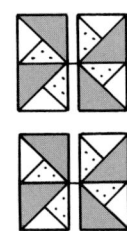

Pressing

The direction that the seams are pressed is important to both the look of the finished block as well as the ease in construction. It's also important to be consistent in pressing, so the blocks can be joined easily later and so the quilting will be the same on all the blocks. We have included pressing diagrams for each block.

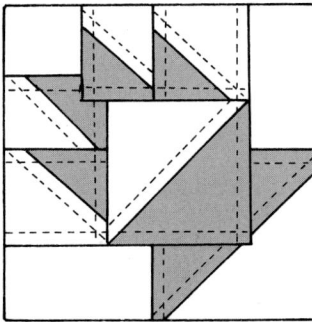 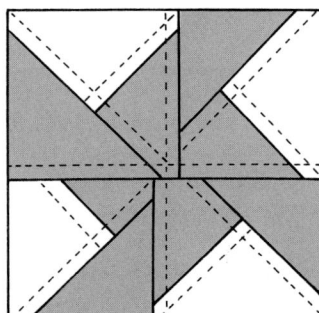

In most cases, the seams are pressed away from the background fabric and toward any points. We like the illusion of foreground and background that this gives. Sometimes this makes matching seams trickier when joining the blocks.

Press on the back, using the iron to guide the seams in place, then turn the piece and lightly press the front.

Appliqué Techniques

Some designs and effects are impossible to achieve in patchwork; only appliqué will accurately render the shape of a flower petal or the curve of a heart. Two different techniques for hand appliqué are presented; choose the one that suits you best.

Templates are made similar to those for piecing. Use pliable template plastic (not acetate) or stiff watercolor paper. Trace the shapes, transferring any marks and grainline arrows. Draw the curves with short, feathery strokes or a series of dots instead of one continuous line. Cut the templates very carefully and smoothly.

Since it's difficult to cut a true circle, we sometimes use other items for a template. A lid from a milk or pill bottle is sometimes close enough to the pattern size that it can be substituted. Circle templates are also available from office or drafting supply stores.

The directions allow for some excess on the background pieces. Handling will cause the fabric to fray and the smaller blocks need extra for ease in working. The pieces will be trimmed to the correct size later.

Press the background, then fold and crease it in quarters. Then make diagonal creases. These aid in placing the appliqué pieces. The placement of the more complicated designs can be lightly marked on the background.

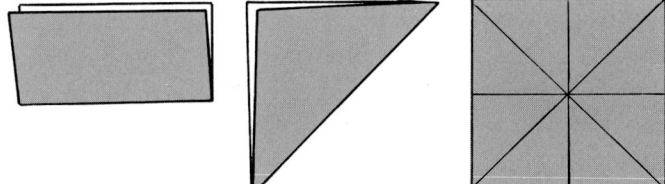

NEEDLE-TURN APPLIQUÉ

The simplest, and probably the oldest, technique for appliqué involves the turning under of the seam allowance as the shape is stitched. The sewing line is marked on the right side of the fabric, and followed exactly. Place the templates with the grainline arrows consistent with the grain of the fabric. This will allow any curves to be on the bias of the fabric, which helps the appliqué be rounded and smooth.

Cutting

Mark around the templates on the right side of the fabric, leaving at least ½ inch between the lines. Use a chalk pencil, or a very sharp colored or regular pencil, and mark with a very fine line. Cut the shapes 3/16 inch from the lines. It may take some practice to cut 3/16 inch instead of the usual ¼ inch seam allowance, but this smaller seam will allow smoother curves. Do not clip the seam allowances except at inside corners and on very tight inside curves.

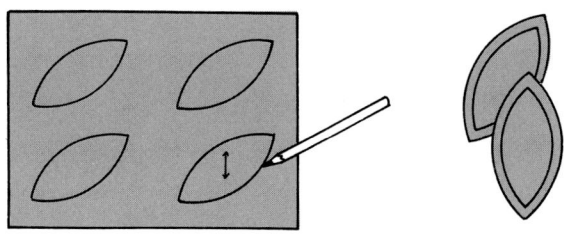

Place the appliqué pieces on the background, using the creases or marks as guidelines. After they are arranged correctly, lift off all but the first piece to be sewn (the appliqué pattern pieces are lettered in working sequence). Pin the shape in place, using small, fine pins or short sequin pins.

Detail pieces are sometimes hard to position without the larger shape in place. These can be inserted while sewing the larger shape. The beaks and feet of the geese, for instance, can be added as the adjacent area is sewn. This is easier than trying to position them correctly without the goose as reference.

Sewing

It's best to use a fine, long needle for this method of appliqué. Sharps, in size 11, are recommended. Use regular sewing thread or fine machine embroidery thread in the color of the appliqué piece. A good match in thread will help the stitches disappear. Always use a single strand no more than 18 inches long.

Start sewing away from any points and very curved areas. Fold under some of the seam allowance, holding it in place with the thumb.

We feel it's easier to handle the seams and control the stitches while facing the edge to be sewn. However, most quilters prefer working with the edge to be sewn facing away from them.

Bring the needle up through the background and just the edge of the fold. Make a stitch straight into the background, catching the edge of the fold as the needle is pulled back out. A tug on the thread will help pull the stitch tight, bringing the fold of the appliqué even closer to the background and making the stitches disappear. There should be eight to twelve stitches per inch.

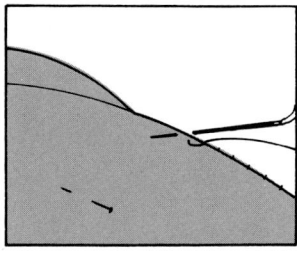 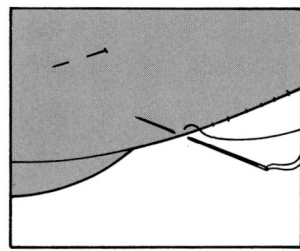

Continue in this manner, folding under the seam on the marked line and holding it with the thumb in front of the needle. The needle should be used to tuck under the seam allowance and to smooth and distribute any fullness. End the stitching by turning the piece over and making an ending knot.

Points and Corners

Nice sharp points can also be achieved with this method. Sew up to the point, then turn under the tip, folding under more than the seam allowance. Pull the thread and bring out the tip of the point. Continue sewing, pushing in the seam allowance at the side of the tip.

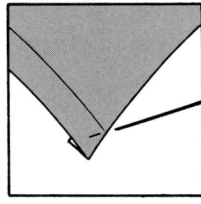 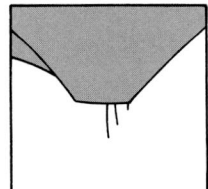 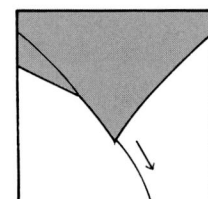

Inside corners should be clipped just before they are sewn. Clip just to the line, then pinch the fabric next to the clip to form a crease. Remove any pins in that area and fold under the entire piece along the line of sewing. Sew to the clip, using the crease as a guide since the actual clip is folded under and cannot be seen. Bring out the rest of the piece, and fold under just the seam allowance again. With an extra stitch at the clip, continue sewing.

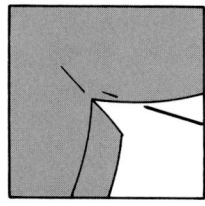 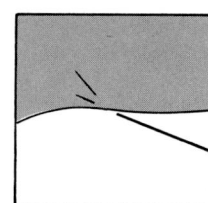 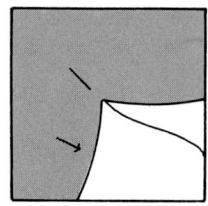

Appliqué Techniques

PAPER BASTE APPLIQUÉ

This method is a variation on the traditional method of first basting under all the seam allowances. Instead of basting the fabric shapes, which sometimes results in bumpy curves and bulky points, the fabric is basted over a construction paper shape. The paper gives a firm edge to the piece, and even beginners have terrific results. It's best to use white or natural colored construction paper since the colors can rub off onto the fabrics.

Cutting and Basting

Make two templates for every shape to be appliquéd; one without seams, as printed in the directions, and one with a true ¼ inch seam allowance. Use the template without seams to cut the pieces from the construction paper. Use the template with seams to cut the pieces from the fabrics. You will need one paper shape for each of the fabric shapes.

Pin a paper shape to the wrong side of a fabric piece. Use a single strand of contrast color thread and baste the seam allowance over the paper, leaving the knot on the right side of the fabric. There may be some extra fullness on outside curves, but instead of clipping, form small gathers or pleats. At corners or points, only the two sides are turned, not the tip. There may be some fabric showing from the front but do not trim. Clip at inside curves and corners to allow the fabric to turn smoothly. If an appliqué piece will be overlapped by another piece, it is not necessary to baste that area. When the shapes are completely basted, end the thread, without knotting, on the right side of the piece.

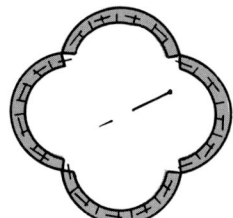 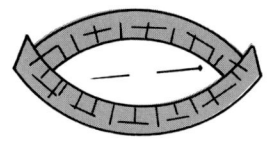

The shapes are appliquéd to the background with the paper still inside. Since the papers are removed just before the appliqué is completed, it is important to begin the stitching on a smooth curve or straight edge. The patterns are lettered for placement order.

Sewing

Thread a needle (sharps, in size 10, 11, or 12) with a single strand of regular thread in a color that matches the appliqué piece. The sewing is done with a ladder stitch; this stitch, combined with a good match in thread color, will make the appliqué stitches virtually invisible. The ladder stitch is done in two steps; one stitch is taken in the background fabric, then one stitch is taken in the appliqué piece. The stitches should be straight (like the rungs of a ladder), not angled. The piece can be held with the edge to be sewn either facing towards or away from you; try it both ways to determine which is the most comfortable.

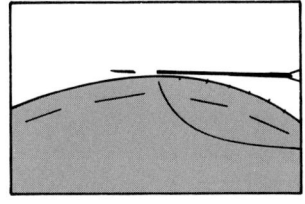 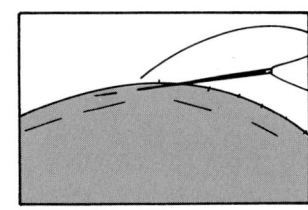

At a corner or point, the excess seam allowance should be flipped to the side away from the line of stitching. Sew to the point, with the last stitch right at the tip. Trim the excess at an angle, then push it under with the needle, towards the side that has already been sewn. It helps to use the side of the needle since the tip can comb through the threads, causing fraying.

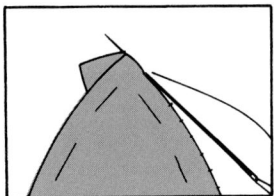 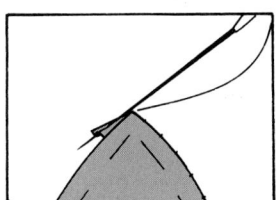

Inside corners, such as the cleft of a heart, need another kind of stitch. Since the fabric has been clipped at inside corners, there is no fold for the stitch to catch. Sew with a tiny whip stitch, catching any stray threads.

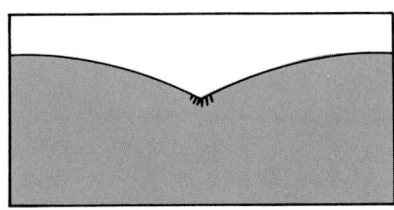

Removing the Papers

When the stitching is within an inch of the starting point, stop and anchor the needle in the fabric. With small, pointed scissors, clip and remove all the basting threads. Lift the seam allowance and grasp the paper with tweezers. With a twisting motion, pull out the paper. Turn the seam allowance back under and finish the appliqué. Bring the thread to the back and knot.

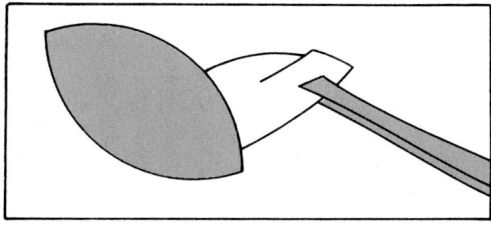

Open ended shapes, such as petals, will have a side that is not basted. After removing the paper from this side, baste the seam allowance in place. This will keep it from shifting later.

CIRCLES

This is an original and easy method of making perfect circles, no matter how tiny. Extra fabric in the seam allowance make the circles look like they have been individually padded. The technique is similar to the paper baste method, but instead of paper, metal washers are used.

Metal washers (round discs with a hole in the center) are available at any hardware store in a multitude of sizes. Be sure to wash them before using. The radius (half the distance across the circle) should be added as the seam allowance on all sides. Use a compass to make a template this size for the fabric circles.

Sewing

With a single strand of matching thread, sew around the edge of the fabric circle, ⅛ to ¼ inch from the edge, with a small running stitch. Be sure to leave the beginning knot on the right side of the fabric. End the stitching on the right side also, but without a knot. Turn the piece over and insert the washer. Pull on the unknotted end of the thread to gather the fabric around the washer. Cut the thread, leaving a 4 inch long tail.

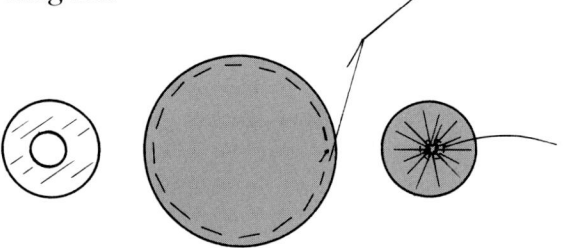

Place the circle in position on the background, with the beginning and ending point of the gathering stitches at the 9 o'clock position on a clock face. Pull the tail of the thread to the 3 o'clock position.

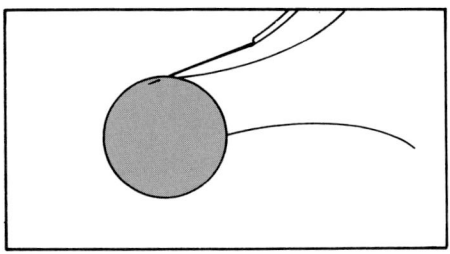

Appliqué the circle, starting the stitching at the 12 o'clock position, and sew in a counter-clockwise direction. (It's easy to hold the circle in position, but it can also be basted in place through the hole in the center.) When the stitching is at the 6 o'clock position, gently loosen the gathering threads and remove the washer. By pulling on the tail of the gathering thread, the seam allowance will be pulled back into place. Finish the appliqué and knot the thread on the back. Trim the tail of the gathering thread by pulling gently and clipping. The thread will then pull back inside the circle.

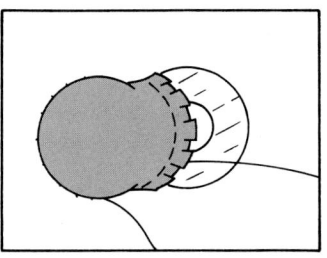 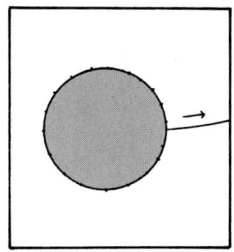

FINISHING THE APPLIQUÉ

Embroider any details on the appliqué pieces using the stitches called for in the quilt directions. After all the stitching is finished, the appliqué piece will need to be pressed. The background may be especially wrinkled from being held so much. Place the appliqué face down on a fluffy towel and press with a dry iron, using a spray of water if necessary. Don't press too hard, or the appliqué pieces will be flattened and the seam allowances will show though them.

Trim the excess fabric, according to the quilt directions. Although some appliqué methods call for the trimming of the background within each shape after the appliqué is complete, we advise against this. We feel it weakens the quilt, and have yet to see an antique quilt on which this was done.

Finishing Techniques

Press each block carefully and consistently. Note any blocks that are different in size than the others. A slightly smaller block can be stretched while pressing; a larger block can be trimmed or reworked, if the size discrepancy is more than a half inch. Always measure blocks across the center since the edges may have stretched. Measure a few blocks to get the average size; this is the measurement to use when cutting any plain squares or sashing pieces.

Use a ruler or the lines on a cutting mat to make sure the blocks are square. Trim any uneven edges or distorted corners. Finally, check the backs of the blocks to make certain that all the seams are sewn in the correct direction. If some seams have been flipped, take the time now to fix them.

ASSEMBLING THE QUILT

Join the blocks in the arrangement specified in the individual quilt directions. Even if the blocks were pieced by hand, assembly can be done by machine, if preferred. The blocks, whether they are placed straight or diagonally, can be chainpieced. Plan for the seams of the blocks to be pressed toward any sashing or setting pieces.

Place the blocks in the correct arrangement. Straight-set blocks are then stacked in vertical rows with the bottom block on the bottom. Sew the first two stacks on the left into pairs of blocks. Leaving the connecting threads, add the blocks from the third stack. Continue adding the blocks until the horizontal rows are formed. The threads connecting the blocks will keep them in position for the horizontal seams.

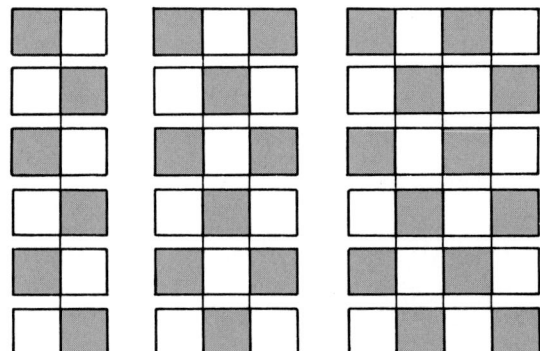

If the blocks have sashing between them, they can still be chainpieced. Treat each sashing piece as if it were the next block. The rows will have to be clipped apart to add the horizontal sashing pieces.

Diagonally-set blocks should also be stacked in rows. However, the rows will not all have the same number of blocks. Stack the blocks, keeping the setting pieces in position. Sew the blocks into rows. Leave the threads connecting the rows and sew the next seams.

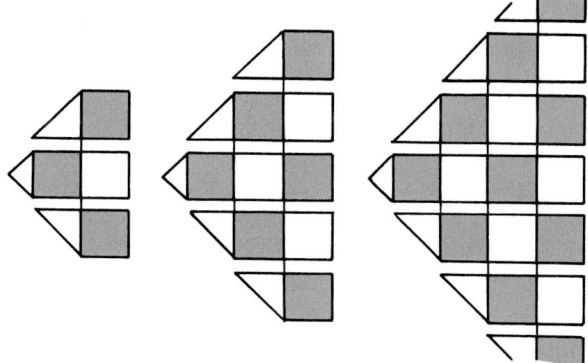

ADDING THE BORDERS

It's important that borders be made to fit each quilt, rather than match the directions. Measure the length and width of the top, measuring across the center since the edges may have been stretched from handling. Compare these measurements to the quilt directions and adjust if necessary. The quilt directions have 2 inches added to each border length. Trim the excess before sewing straight borders. Trim the excess after sewing the corner seam on mitered borders.

Mitered Borders

If there is more than one border, sew them together and add them to the quilt as a unit. Center, then pin and sew the border pieces to all four sides, stopping and starting ¼" from the corners. Fold the quilt top with wrong sides together, aligning the border seams. Fold the borders towards the quilt. Draw a line from the stitching to the raw edge at a 45 degree angle. A triangle ruler is great for this. Pin, then repeat for the other three corners. Sew from the stitching line to the outside edge. Trim the excess fabric and press the seam open.

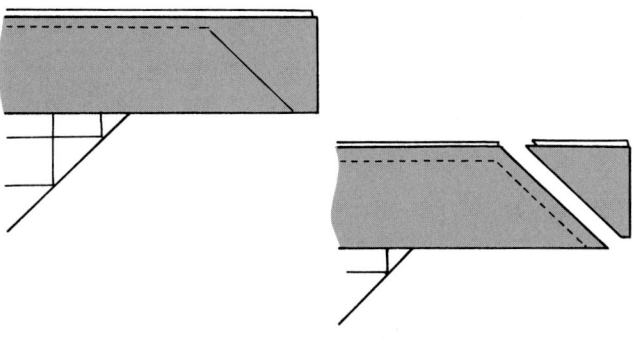

Patchwork Borders

Pieced borders should be measured carefully before attaching them to the quilt. A piece may have to be added or removed to have the border fit. If the border is only slightly different in size (less than the size of one unit), several seams can be sewn with a narrower or wider seam allowance.

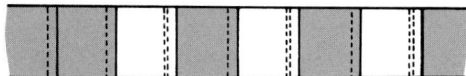

Some of the quilts with patchwork borders also have a plain border. The plain one can be adjusted to make the other fit. Wait to cut the plain border until the pieced one is complete. Place the pieced border next to the quilt to determine the width of the plain border. Attach the plain border, then add the patchwork border.

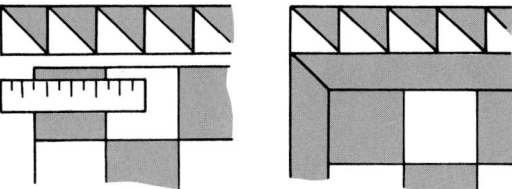

QUILTING

Quilting not only holds the layers of the quilt together, it adds warmth, texture, and beauty. A traditional approach is to outline each patch ¼ inch from the seams. Stitching can also be done along the seam lines, taking care to stay on the side away from the seam allowances. Another style involves ignoring the pattern and covering the surface with a grid, or a series of arcs or swirls.

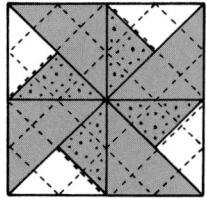 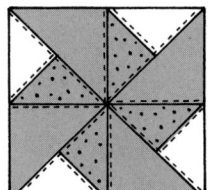 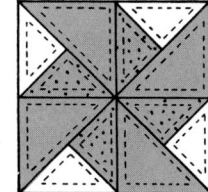

Marking

Some quilting can be done without marking the surface first. Outline stitching simply follows the shape of the patches, either next to the seam or ¼ inch away. Many quilters find it easy to "eyeball" the ¼ inch; others prefer using ¼ inch wide masking tape, which can be lifted and used again, as a guide.

Finishing Techniques

Other designs will have to be marked on the quilt top before quilting can begin. Always use products that are meant for quilts, such as chalk pencils, silver pencils, or water-erasable markers. Be sure to follow the directions and test before using. We've also had good results with needle-marking, where the fabric is creased by the tip of a darning or milliners needle.

Simple shapes can be transferred by making a template of the design, and marking around it. It's also possible to trace a design through the quilt; a light box or sunny window will provide enough light for all but the darkest fabrics. Tape the design in place, position the quilt over it, and trace.

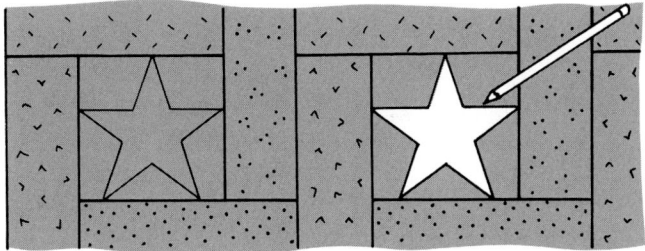

For straight lines or grids, use a ruler as a guide. Instead of trying to measure the distance between the lines, make reference marks on the edge of the piece. Connect these marks for an easy and more accurate set of lines. For diagonal lines on the edge of a quilt, use a 45 degree triangle to insure that the lines stay at the correct angle.

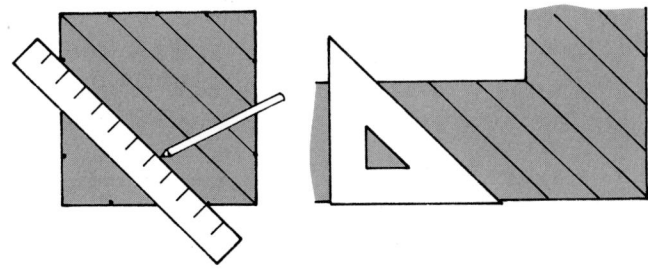

Mark all the quilting designs before basting the layers of the quilt together.

Basting

Press the quilt top a final time. As you press, clip any stray threads on the back. We like to give the quilts a good shaking (like shaking a rug), to rid them of loose threads.

The quilt backing should be 2 or three inches larger than the quilt top on all sides. This is important since the three layers of the quilt can shift during the quilting process. Most of these quilts use only one length of fabric for the backing. Since most printed fabric measures between 41 and 43 inches, any quilt measuring close to 40 inches will require two lengths. There will be excess fabric which can be used for the binding or saved for another project. Trim the selvages before joining the backing lengths. Use a ¼ inch seam allowance and press the seams open to reduce bulk.

A table top is a good surface for basting. Place the backing right side down and masking tape it to the table. Gently spread the batting on top. Add the quilt top, centering it and smoothing out any fullness. Using milliners' needles and light colored thread (quilting thread has less tendency to tangle), make large stitches through all the layers. This can be a simple running stitch or a large whip stitch.

Using long lengths of thread, baste in a grid pattern every four to six inches. Avoid basting exactly where a line of quilting will be. Distribute any fullness evenly; the quilting will ease it in later. Baste the edges of the quilt securely. As a final step, bring the excess backing to the front and baste it in place as a temporary binding. This protects the edges of the quilt and keeps the batting from being tattered.

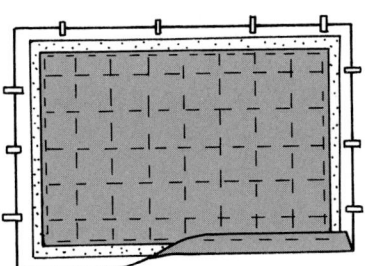

Quilting Tools

Quilting needles, called betweens, are part of the secret behind small, even stitches. Betweens are short needles and this helps create the tiny stitches desired; in fact, the smaller the needle, the smaller the stitch. Use a size from nine to twelve; the higher number indicates the smaller needle. Quilting thread, stronger and more wiry than regular thread, is also less prone to tangling.

The small size of these quilts makes them easy to handle. Quilting hoops, from 12 to 16 inches in diameter, are ideal. Always put on the outer hoop loosely, then tighten it, to avoid distorting the layers. It's always a good idea to try to work from the center area of the quilt outward. This distributes any extra fullness to the outside edges.

The Quilting Stitch

After threading the needle with about 18 inches of thread, tie a small knot. Insert the needle ½ inch from the line of stitching. Bring the needle out on the line, popping the knot through the top into the batting. One hand, with a thimble on the middle finger, pushes the needle into the quilt. The other hand, beneath the quilt, helps direct the needle back to the top of the quilt. Repeat this rocking motion until there are three to five stitches on the needle.

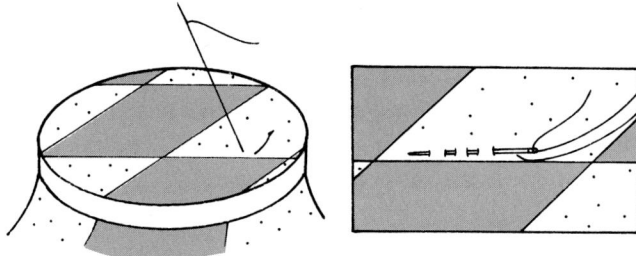

Taking several stitches at a time keeps them even. Try to have the stitches straight and uniform; tiny stitches will come with practice. Stop the stitching with several inches of thread left. Tie a single knot and again pop the knot through the top layer, imbedding the knot between the layers.

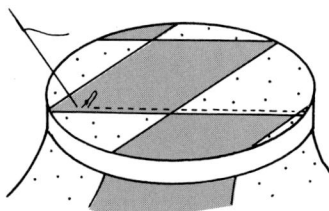

When a line of stitching crosses a seam, it may be difficult to keep the stitches consistent, or even pierce all the layers. Even if a stitch or two does not catch the backing, the quilting will appear consistent if the batting is caught. The only alternative is to take individual stab stitches through the bulky areas.

If the stitching is next to the seamline, stay on the side without the seam allowances. Jog the line of quilting at the seam junctions to keep on the side without the seams. Not only is it difficult to quilt on top of the seam allowances, but the stitches will look different from those in other areas.

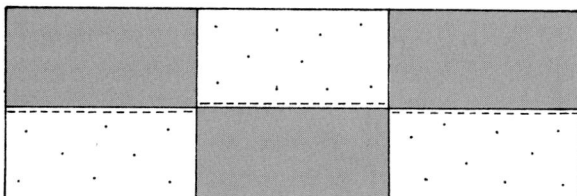

Special Techniques

Pass the needle through the layers to get from one area to another without taking any stitches. If the lines are further apart than a needle's length, it's still possible to do this. Bring just the tip of the needle out and pivot the eye end toward the next area to quilt. Poke the eye end of the needle through the top fabric and pivot the tip toward the next area. Continue to do this, taking care not to bring the needle completely out until you have reached the next line to quilt. Bring the needle completely up and continue to quilt.

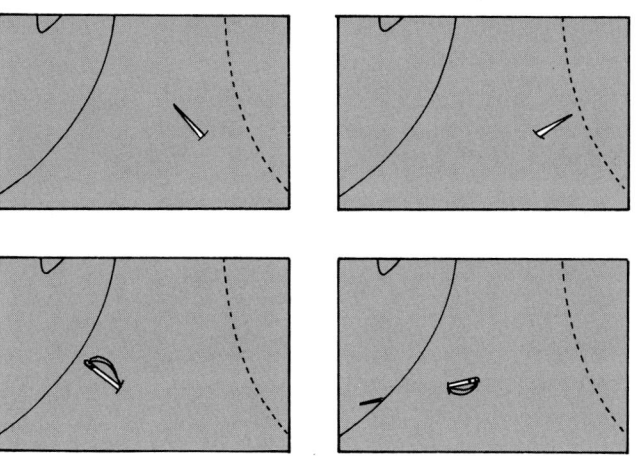

If there is some thread left on the needle after quilting to the edge of the hoop, simply pull out the needle and leave the tail of thread. This tail can be threaded again when the adjacent area is quilted. Some quilters prefer threading several needles, and working on several lines of stitching at a time.

When quilting the edges of the quilt, use the excess backing to help secure the edges to the frame or hoop. Sometimes it is necessary to attach extra strips to help anchor the edges.

Speciality edgings, such as prairie points, are sewn to just the top layer. Stop quilting three or four inches from the edges. Finish the quilting after the edging is added and the backing is sewn to it.

EDGINGS AND FINISHES

The edging of the quilt will serve as both a finish and a frame. We've included an assortment of edgings; feel free to use any of these for your own quilt. The yardages amounts for the edging are listed separately from the fabrics for the quilt. Add extra fabric if your quilt is larger.

Finishing Techniques

Cutting the Binding

A separate, applied binding is the preferred edging of most quilters. The strips are folded in half before attaching, making a double-layer binding. The strips can be cut on the straight or bias grain of the fabric.

Cutting on the bias makes a binding that is nicely rounded, and capable of curving. Because of the angle of the threads, it gives the quilt a longwearing edge.

Square the cut edges of the fabric. Fold the cut edge to the selvage edge to establish the bias. Mark and cut strips (2½ inches wide unless otherwise specified) parallel to the fold. Estimate the number of strips needed by loosely placing them around the quilt as they are cut. Don't cut the entire piece into strips; the excess fabric can be saved for another project and the shorter strips result in too many seams in the binding. Join the strips, as shown, and press the seams open.

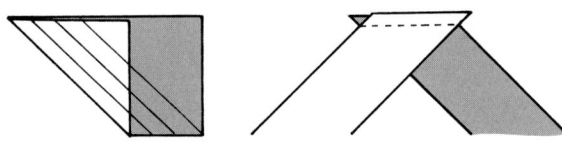

A bias binding can also be cut continuously. Fold a 25 inch square of fabric in half diagonally and press to crease. Cut on the crease to make two triangles. Place the triangles as shown, lining up the top edges. Sew these edges with ¼ inch seam allowances. When the piece is opened, it will form a parallelogram. Press the seam open. On the wrong side, make lines every 2½ inches, starting at a long edge. If the last line is less than 2½ inches from the edge, cut off the excess. Fold the piece as shown, with the first line on the body of the piece aligned with the second line on the tip. Pin and sew, again using a ¼ inch seam. Keeping one hand in the middle of the piece, cut on the marked lines.

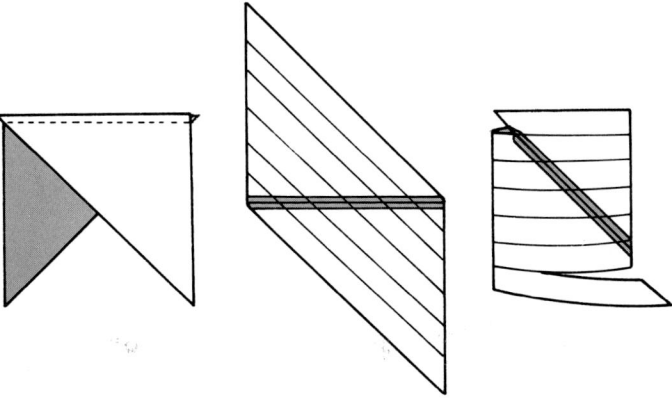

Bindings can be cut on the straight of the grain. This is usually done when the binding fabric is in a long, narrow piece. Cut strips on the crosswise or lengthwise grain (whichever will yield the longer strips). This binding can only be used on straight-edge quilts. Fold the ends of the strips to make a diagonal crease. Sew the strips together along the crease and trim the excess. A diagonal seam reduces bulk and helps disguise the seam.

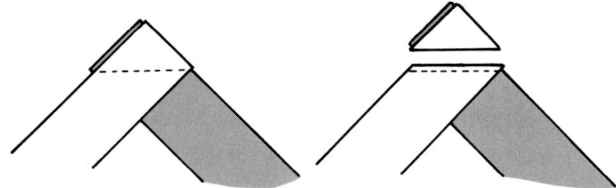

Attaching the Binding

Press the strips in half lengthwise. To keep the bias binding from stretching, staystitch slightly less than ¼ inch from the raw edges. Before attaching, place the binding on the quilt to see where the seams will fall. Seams will be very bulky if they end up exactly at a corner. Move the starting point so this will not happen.

It's best to start the binding on the bottom edge, about ten inches from the corner. There are different ways to start and end the binding. The ends can be left free and seamed together later. The binding can be folded off the edge of the quilt and the end overlapped. A seam allowance can also be turned under at the beginning and the end overlapped.

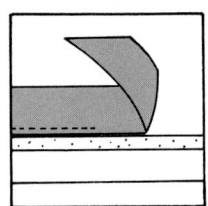 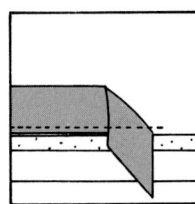 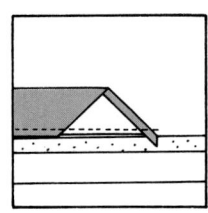

Sew the binding to all three layers of the quilt. Stop stitching ¼ inch from the corner and backstitch. Lift the presser foot and needle and form a ¼ inch pleat. Insert the needle and pivot the quilt. Continue sewing the binding to the quilt, forming a pleat in each corner.

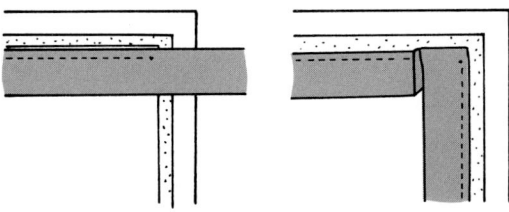

Some quilters prefer rounded instead of pleated corners. The binding must be cut on the bias to do this. Simply curve the binding around each corner, easing as it is sewn. Scalloped edges are treated the same way, with the quilt clipped at the inside points.

After the binding is sewn to the quilt, trim the excess batting and backing. Leave enough batting to lightly pad the binding. Bindings cut 2½ inches wide will need ½ to ¾ inch of excess batting left in place. Fold the binding to the back of the quilt and sew by hand with a blind stitch. For pleated corners, form a matching pleat on the back and stitch in place.

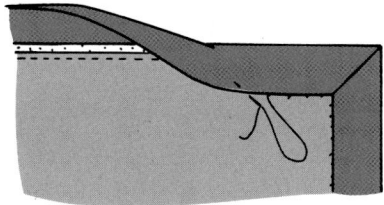

Pieced Binding
Sewing different fabrics together before cutting the bias strips makes a wonderful, candy-stripe binding. Strips 2½ inches wide were used in the binding for Pat-a-Cake, but various widths could also be used. Sew the strips side by side, and press the seams open to reduce bulk. Cut bias strips and join end to end. Fold and press the binding in half, then attach it to the quilt as described above.

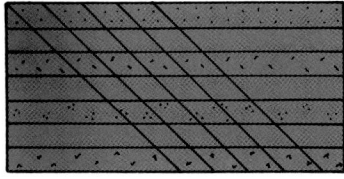 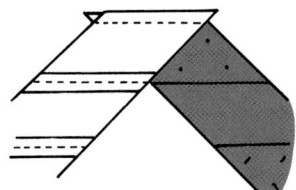

Piping
Piping is similar in look to a bias binding, but with a much more delicate effect. Purchased piping can be used but a better match is possible if you make your own. Cut bias strips 1½ inch wide and seam the ends together. Fold in half lengthwise and sew using a zipper foot, encasing purchased cotton cording. Try not to stretch the strips while sewing. Trim the seam to ¼ inch.

Attach the piping, sewing through the top and batting only, again using a zipper foot. Begin and end by angling the piping off the edge. The piping can also be opened and joined with a diagonal seam.

Trim off the excess fabric and batting. From the backing, trim all but a seam allowance. Sew the backing to the piping by hand, turning under the seam allowance. Finish any quilting along the edges.

Clean Finish
A clean finished edge is used where there is no need for an additional border effect, or where the edge is mostly angles and corners, making most binding methods difficult. Stop the quilting several inches away from the edges and trim all but a seam allowance from all the layers of the quilt. Turn the seam allowances in towards each other and pin frequently. Sew by hand, using a whip stitch. Finish any quilting along the edges.

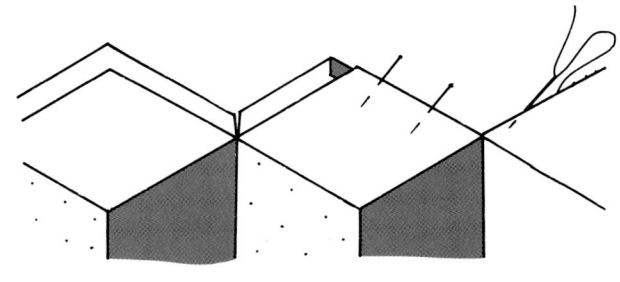

Prairie Points
A fun and easy edging, prairie points add interest, as well as reinforce any triangle shapes in the quilt. They are made by folding squares of one or more fabrics. Fold and press the squares diagonally. Fold and press again to form the points. These are tucked inside each other to create the edging.

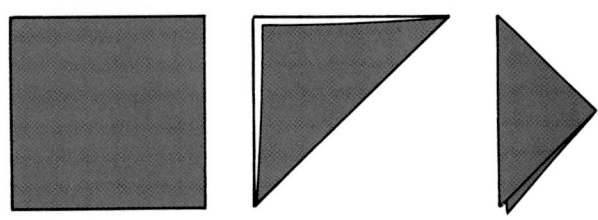

Finishing Techniques

Leave the outer three inches unquilted and pin the points to the quilt top only. Start at the corner, and tuck each prairie point inside the open end of the previous one. The tips of every other point will touch. Adjust the spacing to make the points end at each corner. Sew to the quilt top, making sure all the layers of the prairie points are stitched.

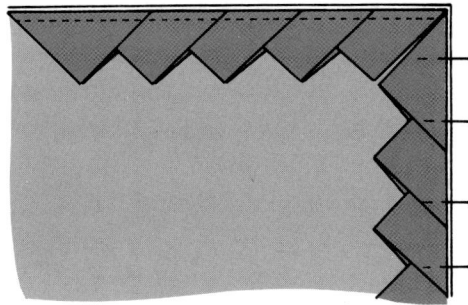

Leave the prairie points flat against the quilt top while trimming the excess batting and backing. Whip stitch the batting to the seam allowance along the edge. Attach the edges of the backing to the prairie points by hand, using a blind stitch. Finish any quilting along the edges.

Scalloped Edging

This is a delightful finish for a quilt and very easy to do. A pattern is included in the Dancing Fans directions. Trace the oval on rectangles of fabric. Place these right sides together with matching pieces. Sew on the marked lines. Cut in half on the center line, then trim the seams on the curved edges to a scant ¼ inch. Turn right side out and press. Pin the scallops to the quilt top, with the scallops touching.

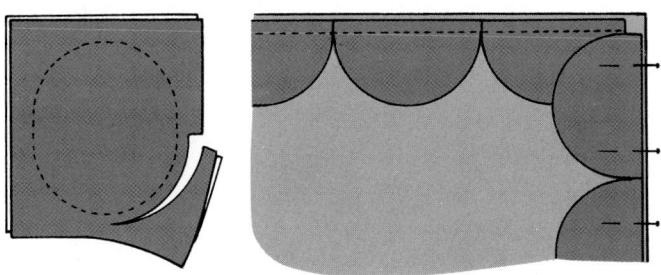

A different quilt might need a different size of scallop. Draw a circle that fits the sides of the quilt evenly. Cut the circle in half and add ½ inch to the center. This forms the oval pattern piece. Trace and sew on the fabric as described above.

CARE AND USE OF THE QUILT

Add a fabric sleeve to the back of the quilt if it will be displayed on the wall. Cut a strip of coordinating fabric the width of the quilt, plus an inch, and nine inches wide. Hem the short ends, then sew the long sides together. With the seam in the center, pin the sleeve to the back of the quilt. Allowing some slack for the rod, handstitch the sleeve to the backing of the quilt. Use a flat wood strip to hang the quilt.

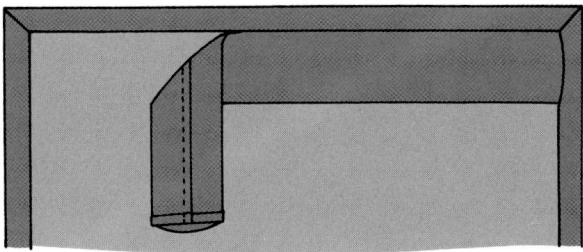

To launder the quilt, use a mild detergent in the washing machine. Don't let the machine agitate since that can break quilting stitches. Instead, use your hands to gently move the quilt through the suds. The spin cycle does not hurt the quilt.

SIGNING THE QUILT

Adding the baby's name, birth date, birth weight and length, and parents' names in embroidery or ink will make the quilt a special keepsake. Use the center of a block or incorporate the information into the design. The inscription could be added to the individual puffs of smoke coming from the train in Railroad Crossing, for example.

However it is done, be sure to add your name and the date the quilt was made. There is always the chance that the quilt will be so appreciated and loved by its little owner that it won't last beyond the childhood years. Hopefully, the quilt will be rescued in time for future generations to cherish.

Rockabye Baby

These are the treetops for baby's cradle, adapted from the traditional Pine Tree block. Solid colors are paired with a print background but prints for the trees on a plain fabric would look as sweet. The Grid Triangle piecing technique makes this quilt a breeze!

41"x55" 7½" blocks
Shown in color on page 33.

Fabric Amounts
Trees and narrow border (purple) – 1½ yards
Trees (green, pink, blue, and yellow solids) –
⅜ yard each
Background (print) – 3 yards
Backing – 3⅓ yards (2 – 60" lengths)
Binding (print) – ¾ yard

Cutting
From purple, cut 2 border pieces 1½"x48" and
  2 pieces 1½"x37". Use the remaining for trees.
From purple, green, and pink solids, cut 48 A*,
  4 C and 4 E each.
From blue and yellow solids, cut 36 A*, 3 C and
  3 E each.
From background, cut 2 pieces 4½"x43" and
  2 pieces 4½"x57".
From the remaining background, cut 216 A*, 72 B,
  18 D, 18 Dr, 10 F and 4 G.
*For Grid Triangle piecing, do not cut A.

Grid Triangles
Mark 24 squares 2⅜"x2⅜" on the purple, green, and pink solids. Pair with the background to make 48 triangle-squares from each.
  Mark 18 squares 2⅜"x2⅜" on the blue and yellow solids. Pair with the background to make 36 triangle-squares from each.

Sewing
Sew and press as shown. If Grid Triangle piecing was used, the A triangles are already sewn into squares. Make 4 blocks each from green, pink, and purple fabrics and 3 blocks each from blue and yellow fabrics, for a total of 18 blocks.

Assembly
Arrange the blocks according to the photograph and diagram. Sew into diagonal rows, with the background triangles at the ends. Center and sew the purple and print border pieces together. Sew to the quilt and miter the corners.

Finishing
Mark and quilt random swirls and curves over the surface of the quilt. Bind to finish.

Rockabye Baby

Sewing

Pressing

Make 18

F: Cut 11⅞" square

G: Cut 6¼" square

A: Cut 2⅜" square

B: Cut 2" square

E: Cut 3½" square

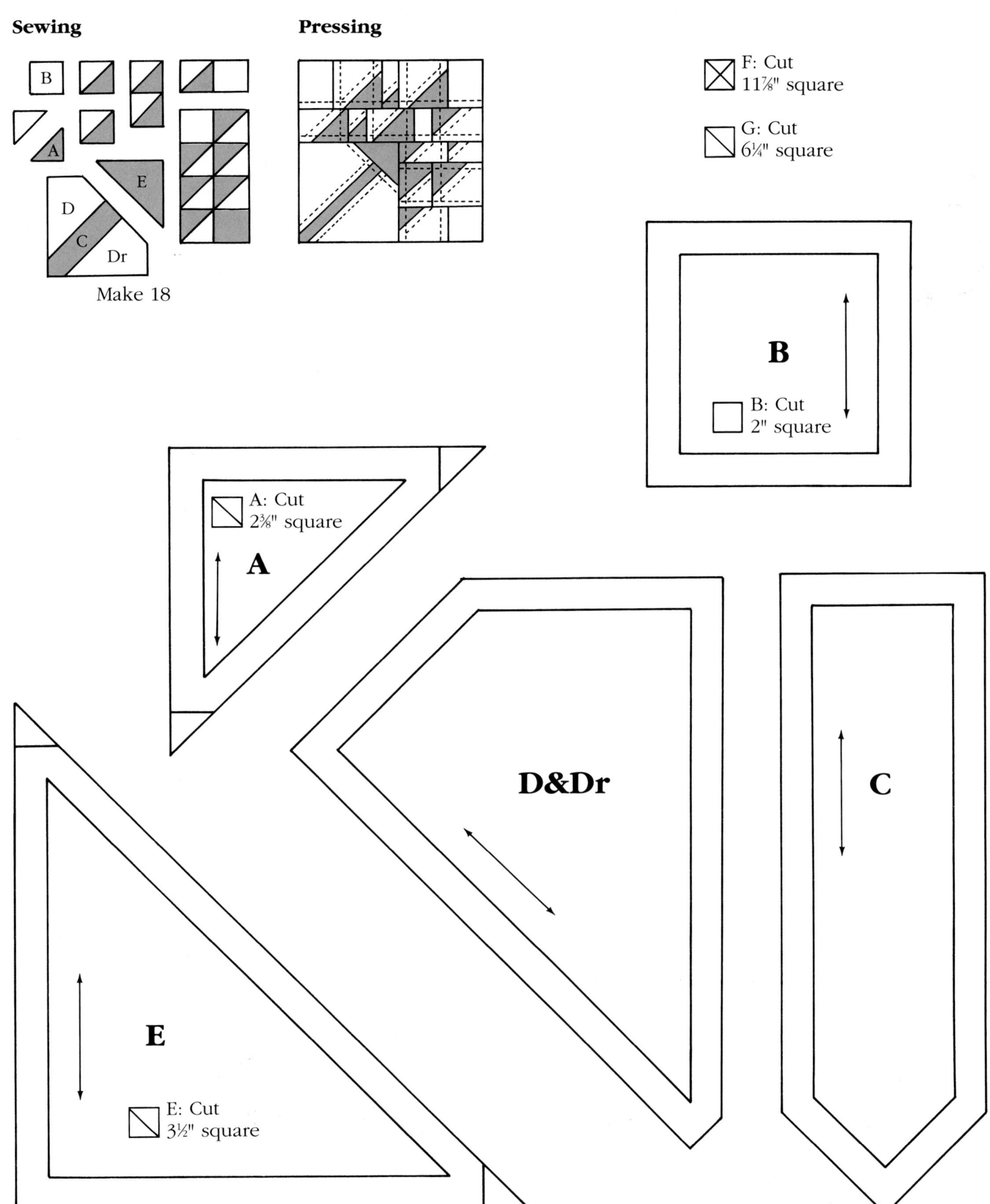

Ring Around the Rosey

A pocketful of posies are appliquéd on a beautiful quilt for cradle or wall. The garland is a perfect frame for baby's name or initials. Elegant quilting designs make this quilt a special gift for that special little someone.

44"x44"
Shown in color on page 33.

Fabric Amounts
Background (white moiré print) – 2½ yards
Buds (deep purple) – ⅛ yard
Stems and leaves (teal) – ¾ yard
Petals (purple) – ⅓ yard
Centers (yellow) – ⅛ yard
Backing – 3 yards (2 – 54" lengths)
Piping (purple) – ¾ yard, plus 6 yards cotton cording, ¼" in diameter

Cutting
From background, cut 4 pieces 10"x44", 1 piece 19" square, and 1 piece 20" square. Cut the larger square diagonally twice.
From deep purple, cut 24 A.
From teal, cut 4 B, 4 Br, 4 C, 4 Cr, 4 D, 4 Dr, 40 E and 36 Er. Also from teal, cut 4 bias strips 1"x8".
From purple, cut 60 F.
From yellow, cut 12 G.

Sewing
Fold and press the bias strips in thirds lengthwise for stems. Fold and crease the center square diagonally. Lightly mark a circle 11" in diameter in the center. Fold and crease the triangles and borders in half. Center the appliqué on the creases.

Complete the appliqué in order: the buds, sepals, stems, leaves, petals and centers. Use the placement marks on the pattern pieces for positioning the sepals and leaves. The center design is rotated a quarter-turn. Trim the center square to 17½", the triangles to 12½" (on the right-angle sides), and the borders to 8½" wide.

Assembly
Add the side triangles to the center, pressing the seams toward the triangles. Add the borders, mitering the corners, and pressing the seams toward the borders.

Finishing
Mark and quilt the feather and grid designs, except for the outer edges. Make the piping as described in the text. Mark the scallops and attach the piping before trimming the excess fabric. Sew the piping to the top and batting, as described in the text. Trim the backing, allowing for the seam. Hand sew the backing to the piping, clipping at the inside angles. Quilt the feather designs in the outside scallops.

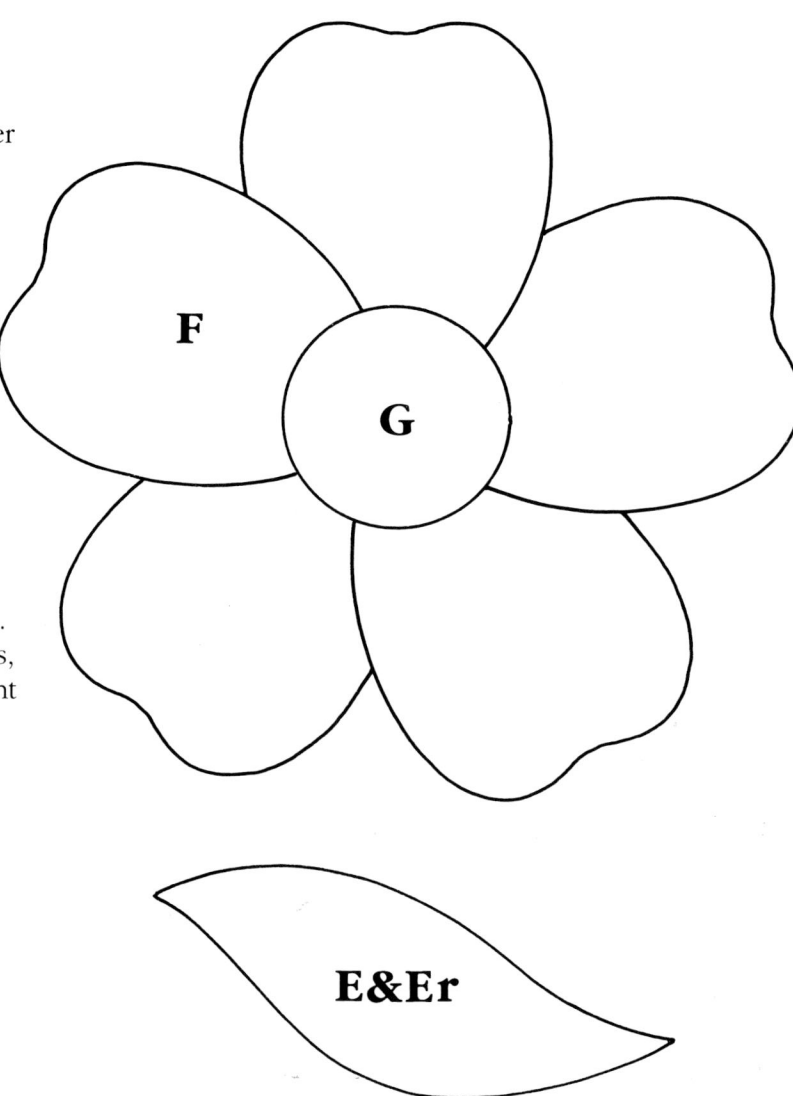

Ring Around the Rosey 31

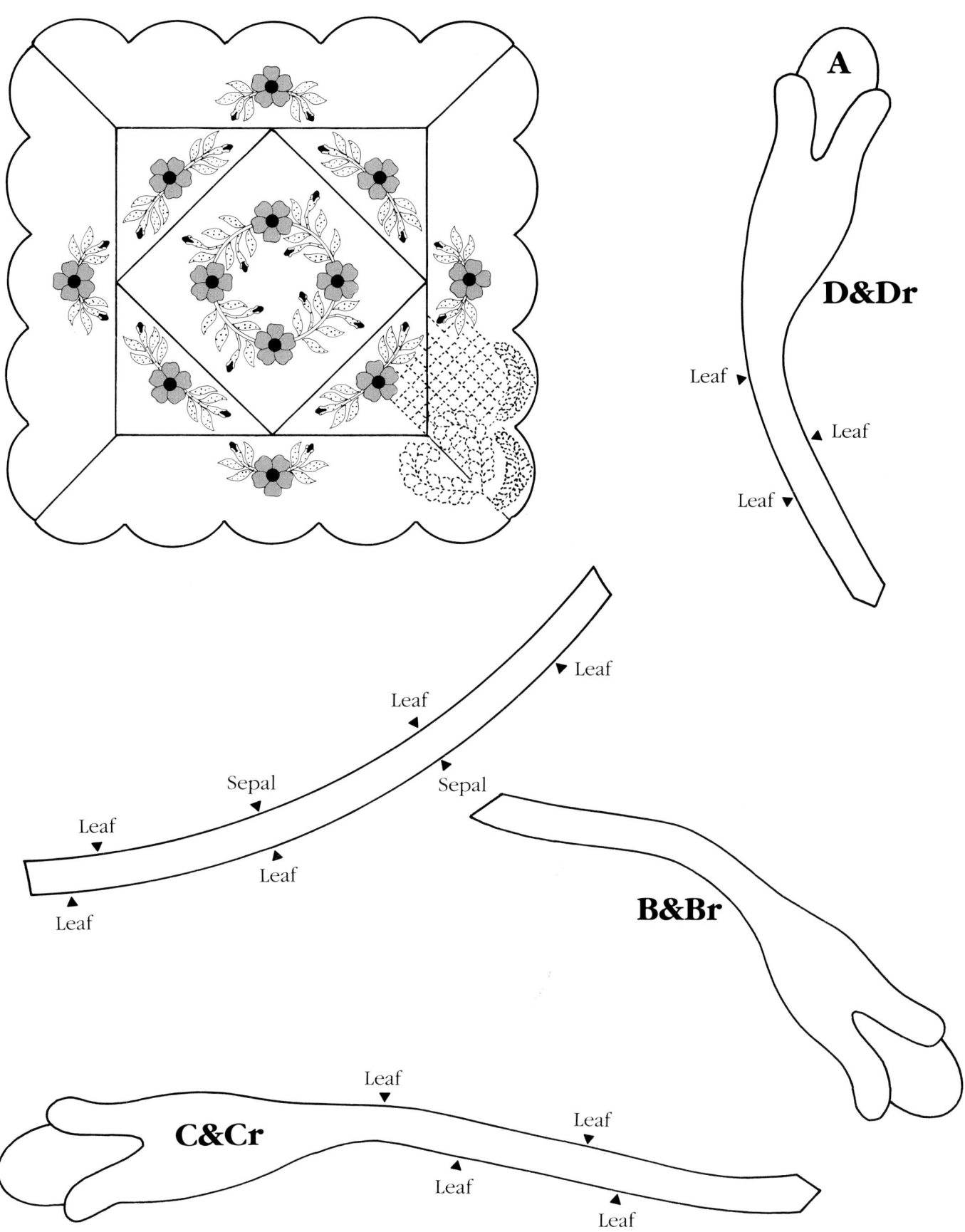

Scallop

Ring Around the Rosey by Deborah Gordon. 44"x44". Hand appliquéd, hand quilted, cotton batting.

Rockabye Baby by Deborah Gordon. 41"x55". Machine pieced, hand quilted, cotton-poly batting.

Night and Noon by Helen Frost. 35"x43". Machine pieced, hand quilted, polyester batting.

Good Morning, Sunshine! *by Helen Frost. 42"x50". Hand appliquéd, machine pieced, hand quilted, cotton-poly batting.*

Baby Blocks *by Deborah Gordon. 35"x46". Hand pieced (paper piecing method), hand quilted, cotton-poly batting.*

Dancing Fans by Deborah Gordon. 30"x42". Machine pieced, hand quilted, polyester batting.

Pat-a-Cake by Deborah Gordon. 40"x46". Machine pieced, hand quilted, cotton-poly batting.

Daisy Chain by Helen Frost. 33"x45". Machine pieced, hand appliquéd, hand quilted, polyester batting.

Little Gosling Chase by Helen Frost. 38"x51". Machine pieced, hand appliquéd, hand quilted, cotton-poly batting.

Sweet Hearts by Helen Frost. 30"x35". Hand appliquéd, hand quilted, polyester batting.

Ribbon Twist by Deborah Gordon. 33"x40". Machine pieced, hand quilted, polyester batting.

Twinkle, Twinkle by Deborah Gordon. 39"x54". Hand pieced, hand quilted, cotton-poly batting.

Bright Hopes by Helen Frost. 33"x39". Machine pieced, hand quilted, polyester batting.

Duck and Ducklings by Helen Frost. 41"x49". Machine pieced, hand appliquéd, hand quilted, polyester batting.

Baby Bunting by Deborah Gordon. 36"x48". Hand pieced, hand quilted, wool batting.

Railroad Crossing by Deborah Gordon. 39"x50". Machine pieced, hand appliquéd, hand quilted, cotton-poly batting.

Whiligig by Helen Frost. 36"x48". Machine pieced, hand quilted, polyester batting.

Night and Noon

Let a special baby snuggle under a starry quilt during nighttime slumber or noontime naps. The blocks create a secondary design which is carried into the border. Add quilted stars to make this a stellar gift for a newborn.

35"x43"   7½" blocks
Shown in color on page 33.

Fabric Amounts
Block center (yellow star print) – ⅓ yard
Star points (dark periwinkle) – ⅝ yard
Star background (yellow print) – ¾ yard
Star background (pink print) – ⅓ yard
Star background and border triangles
   (aqua print) – ½ yard
Star background and border triangles
   (peach print) – ¾ yard
Border (medium periwinkle) – ½ yard
Backing – 1½ yards
Binding (dark periwinkle) – ¾ yard

Cutting
From yellow star fabric, cut 20 A.
From dark periwinkle, cut 160 B.
From second yellow print, cut 80 B and 80 D.
From pink print, cut 80 C.
From aqua print, cut 80 C for blocks and 40 C
   for borders.
From peach print, cut 80 D for blocks and 40 D
   for borders.
From medium periwinkle print, cut 18 E and 4 F.

Sewing
Sew and press as shown. Place the corner triangles on the bottom while sewing to keep the bias edge from distorting. Make 20 blocks.

Sew the remaining peach and aqua pieces together. Join to the E pieces, making 5 units each for the side borders and 4 units each for the top and bottom borders, adding the corner pieces at the ends.

Assembly
Sew the blocks into 5 rows with 4 blocks in each. Attach the side borders, then add the top and bottom borders. Press the seams toward the borders.

Finishing
Outline quilt the diagonal lines of the blocks. Quilt stars in the center squares. Extend the quilting lines into the border. Bind to finish.

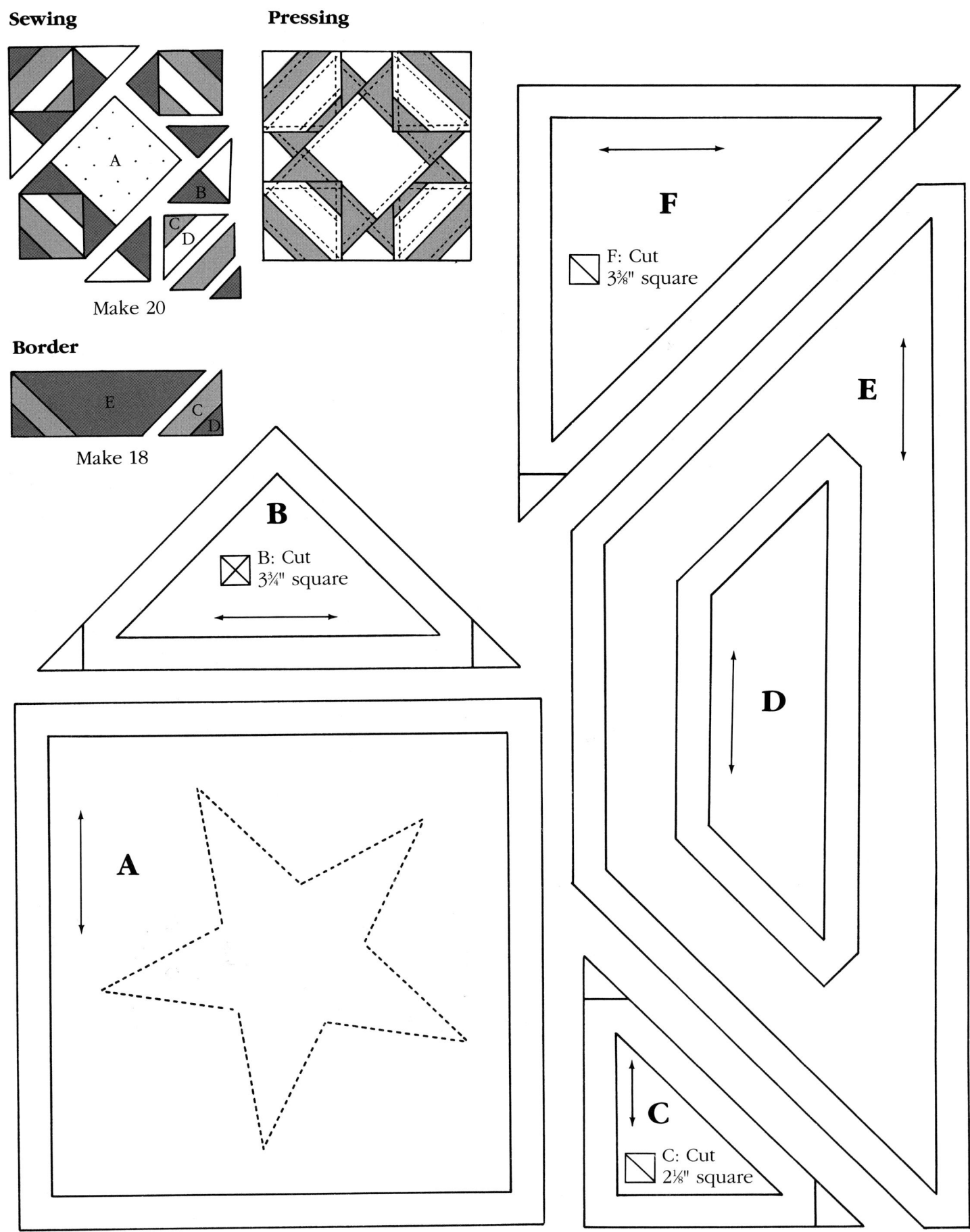

Baby Blocks

This classic quilt pattern is made soft and sweet with a trio of pastel prints. Keep the lightest color on the top of each block and medium and dark for the sides. This will reinforce the illusion of depth. Use paper piecing for a terrific take-along project.

35"x46"   3⅜" blocks
Shown in color on page 34.

Fabric Amounts
Lightest diamonds (yellow) – 1 yard
Medium diamonds (pink) – 1 yard
Darker diamonds (aqua) – 1 yard
Backing – 1½ yards

Cutting
From yellow, pink, and aqua, cut 143 A each.
For paper piecing, cut 429 A (without seams) from construction paper.

Sewing
For hand or machine sewing: Sew as shown, stitching only on the sewing line and setting in the third piece in every block. Make 143 blocks.

For paper piecing, baste the fabric pieces onto the paper pieces and join with a whipstitch as described in the text.

Assembly
Join the blocks into rows. Make 8 rows with 10 blocks in each and 7 rows with 9 blocks in each. Alternate the rows, beginning and ending with the longer rows. Sew the rows together, seaming with hand or machine piecing or whipstitching with paper piecing.

Finishing
Quilt ¼" from the outside of each block. Use the clean finish edging, as described in the text, clipping the backing at the inside angles. Finish the quilting along the outside edges.

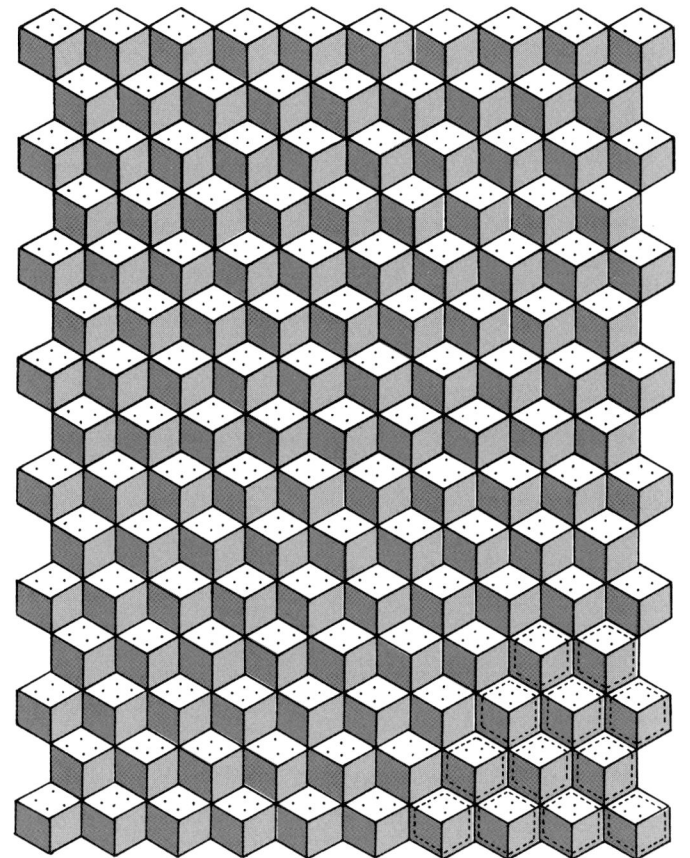

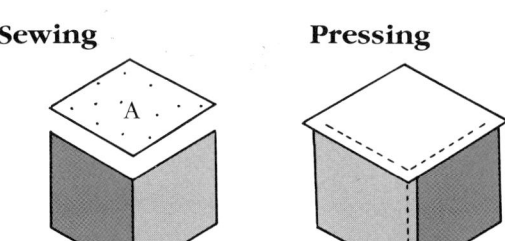

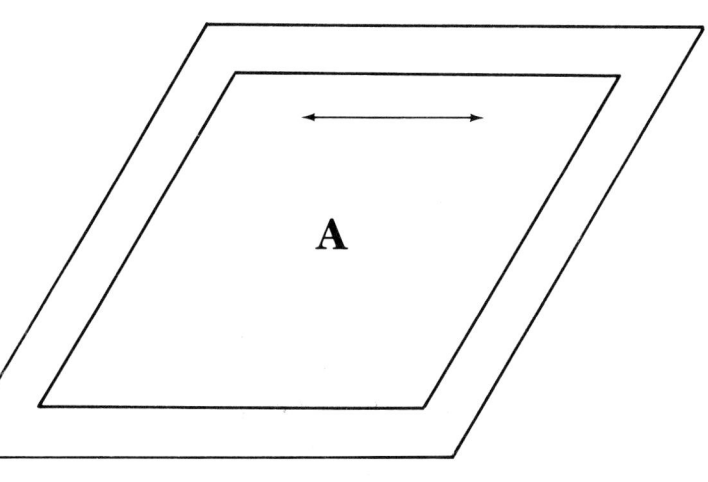

Good Morning, Sunshine!

The sun's first rays streak across the rosy morning sky in this variation of the Moon Over the Mountain quilt pattern. Ten different combinations of pink, aqua, and yellow fabrics were used but fewer would look just fine. Most of the appliqué is on straight edges, making this a simple project that's lots of fun.

42"x50"   6" blocks
Shown in color on page 34.

Fabric Amounts
Background (pinks) – 10 fabrics, ¼ yard each
Mountain (aquas) – 10 fabrics, ¼ yard each
Sun and rays (yellows) – 10 fabrics, ¼ yard each
Setting and borders (white) – 1½ yard
Binding – ¾ yard or use excess from setting fabric
Backing – 3⅛ yards (2 – 56" lengths)

Cutting
From pink fabrics, cut 3 A and 4 G each.
From yellow fabrics, cut 3 B, 3 Br, 3 C, 3 Cr, 3 D, 3 E, and 4 G each.
From aqua fabrics, cut 3 F and 4 G each.
From white fabric, cut 24 pieces 2"x6½", 7 pieces 2"x36", and 2 pieces 2"x45".
Note: Patterns B, C, D, E, and F are appliqué patterns.

Sewing
Fold and crease the pink background squares diagonally and into fourths. The dotted lines on the pattern pieces align with the creases. Hand appliqué the sides of the rays (B, Br, C, Cr, and D), then the sun (E), and then the sides of the mountain (F). Leave the ends of the rays and the bottom of the mountains flat and baste in place. Make 3 blocks with each fabric combination for a total of 30 blocks.

Make the borders by sewing the small squares into 2 rows of 28 squares each and 2 rows of 31 squares each.

Assembly
Sew the short setting pieces between the blocks with 5 blocks in each row. Measure the rows and adjust the length of the longer setting pieces. Sew the 7 longer pieces between and at the ends of the rows. Sew the 2 longest pieces on the sides after measuring and adjusting the length, if necessary.

Sew the longer rows of squares to the sides of the blocks, then add the shorter rows of squares to the top and bottom. Machine staystitch the outer edges of the quilt top, to keep the seams on the squares from opening.

Finishing
Outline the rays, suns and mountains with quilting. Quilt the setting pieces ⅜" from the seams. Use the excess white fabric to cut straight strips for the binding or use another piece for bias binding. Bind to finish.

Good Morning, Sunshine!

Sewing

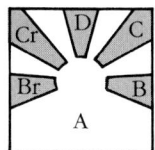 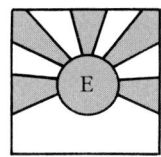 

Make 30

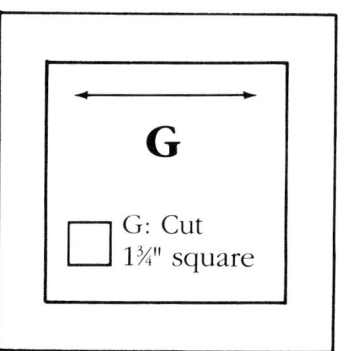

G: Cut 1¾" square

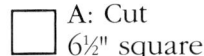

A: Cut 6½" square

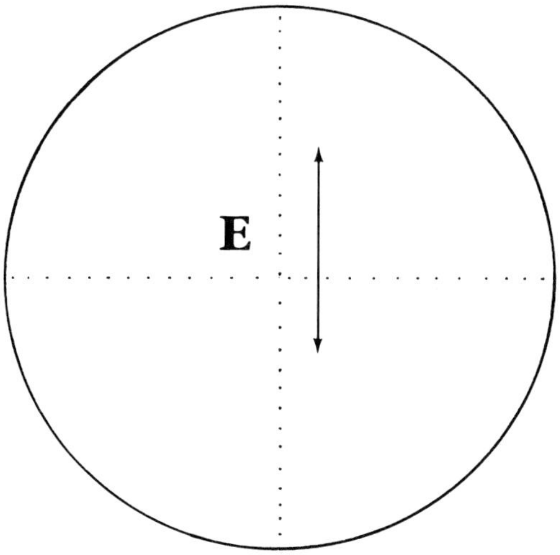

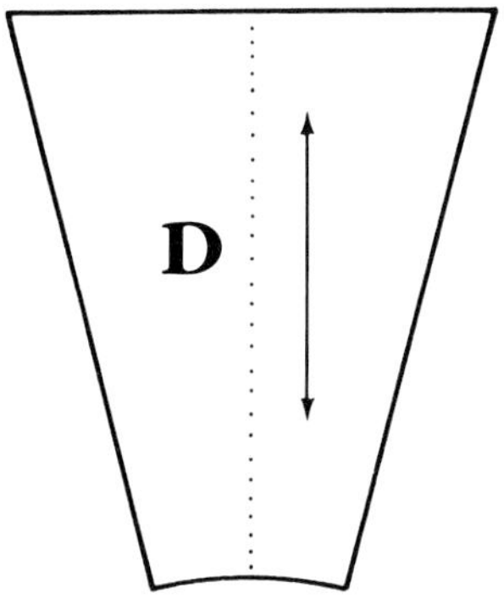

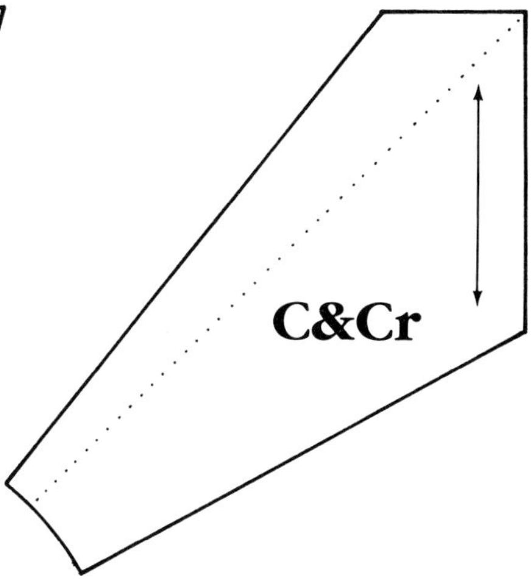

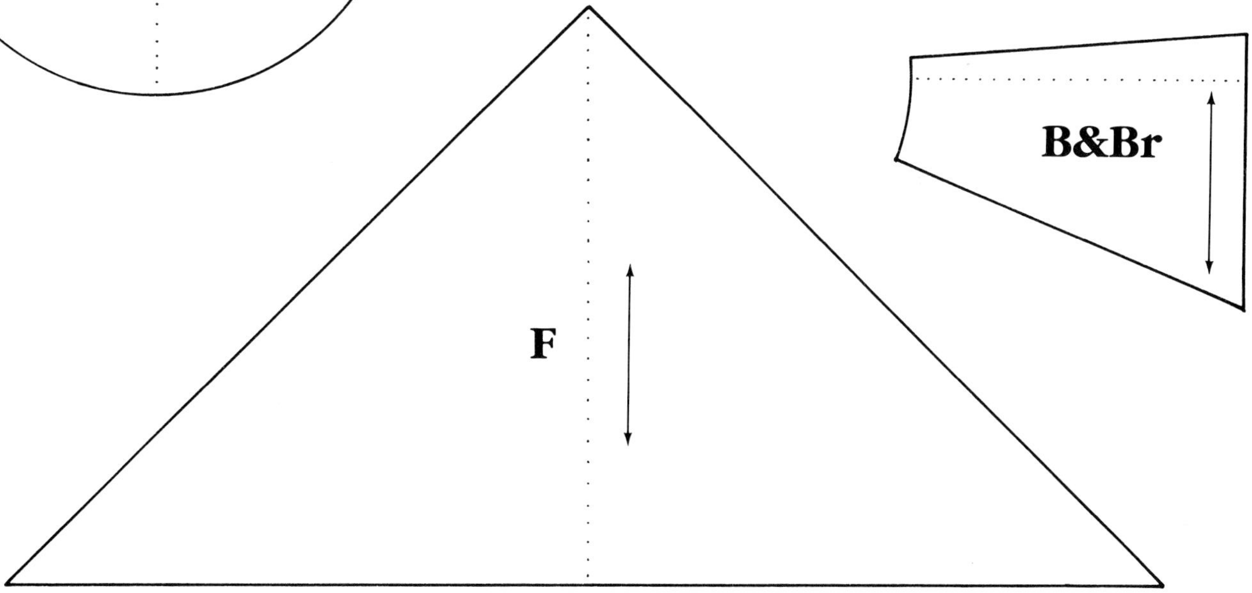

Dancing Fans

This little fan design becomes even fancier with a scalloped edging. Two colors are used, with four shades of each forming the fans. The blocks are arranged to form a diagonal design. Use hand or machine piecing techniques.

30"x42"   6" blocks
Shown in color on page 35.

Fabric Amounts
Fan blades (pale peach and green) – 2 fabrics, ⅓ yard each
Fan blades (light peach and green) – 2 fabrics, ⅓ yard each
Fan blades (medium peach and green) – 2 fabrics, ⅜ yard each
Center fan blades (dark peach and green) – 2 fabrics, ⅜ yard each
Fan handle (darkest green) – ⅝ yard
Scalloped edging (peach and green print) – ⅞ yard
Backing – 1⅜ yards

Cutting
From pale peach, cut 17 A and 17 Ar.
From pale green, cut 18 A and 18 Ar.
From light peach, cut 17 B and 17 Br.
From light green, cut 18 B and 18 Br.
From medium peach, cut 17 C and 17 Cr.
From medium green, cut 18 C and 18 Cr.
From dark peach, cut 17 D.
From dark green, cut 18 D.
From darkest green, cut 35 E.
From peach and green print, cut 48 F.
Mark pattern piece G on 24 of the F pieces.

Sewing
Sew as shown. Press the seams toward the longest blade. Sew the fan to the center piece E, pinning and matching the marks to each seam. Place the fan on top, for ease in sewing. Make 17 peach and 18 green blocks, for a total of 35 blocks.

Assembly
Arrange the blocks according to the photograph and diagram. Make 7 rows, with 5 blocks in each.

Finishing
Outline the blades and center of the fan with quilting next to the seams. Sew and attach the scallops as described in the text.

Sewing

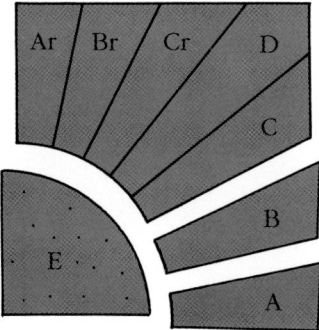

Make 35

Pressing

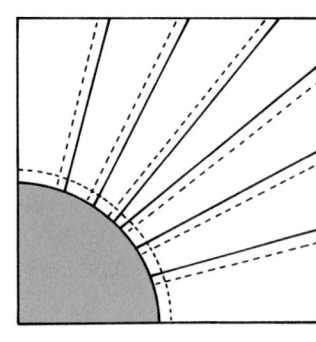

Dancing Fans

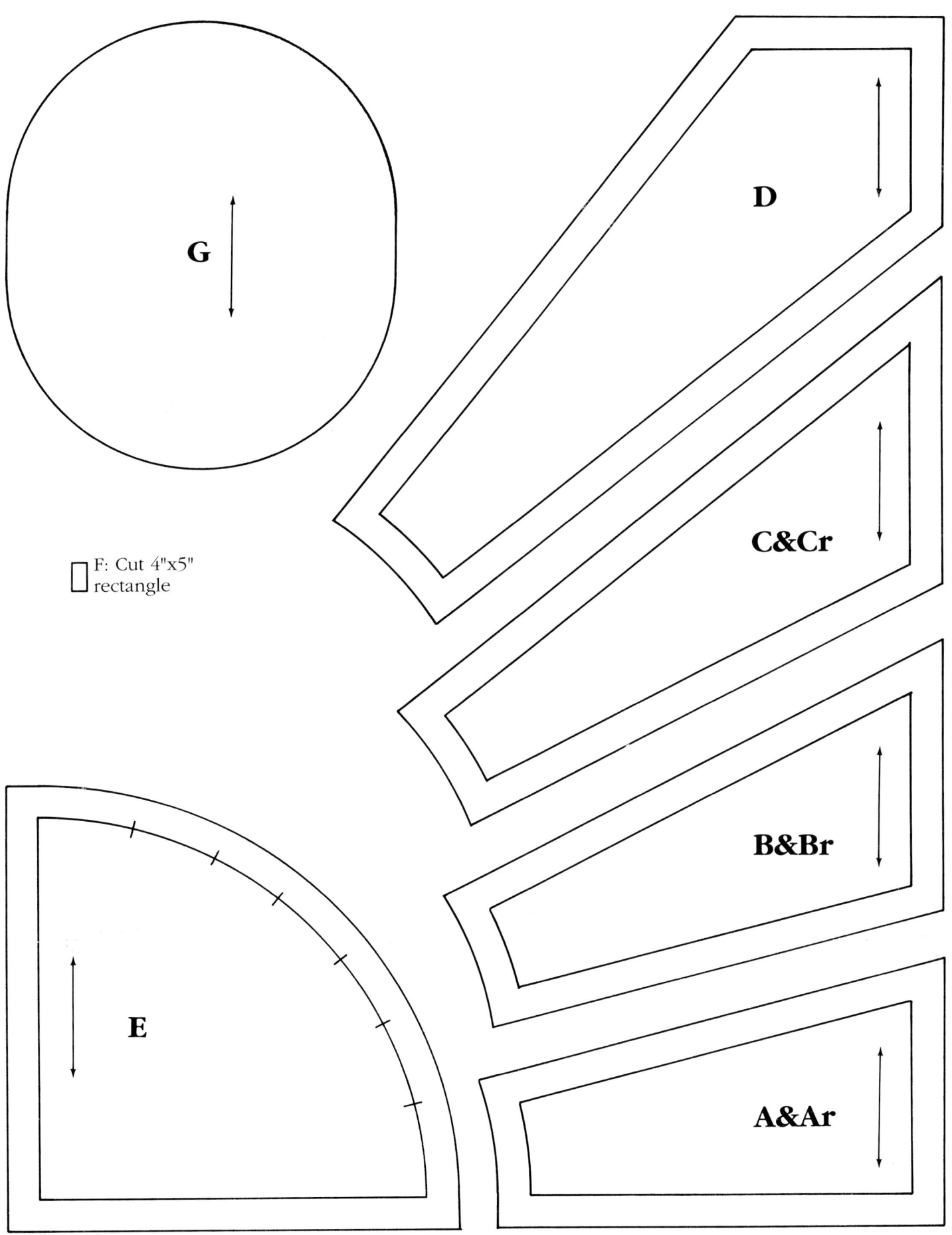

Pat-a-Cake

Lots of little triangles are used to make this small version of the Cake Stand block. The floral fabric adds interest to the background areas. Tiny handprints are quilted in the border to make this a special quilt "for baby and you"!

40"x46"   5" blocks
Shown in color on page 35.

Fabric Amounts
Blocks and border (blue, green, aqua, purple, pink, yellow, and apricot prints) – 7 fabrics, ½ yard each
Background (floral print) – 3 yards
Backing – 1½ yards
Binding – Included in above amounts or ⅛ yard each of 7 fabrics if purchased separately.

Template Cutting
From blue, green, aqua and purple prints, cut 45 A and 5 B each.
From pink, yellow, and apricot prints, cut 39 A and 4 B each.
From each of the above prints, cut 1 strip 2½"x44" for the pieced binding.
From background print, cut 2 pieces 5½"x42" and 2 pieces 5½"x48".
From the remaining background, cut 230 A, 64 B, 32 C, 64 D, 14 E, and 4 F.

Grid Triangle Cutting
Mark 18 squares 2⅛"x2⅛" on each of the print fabrics. Pair with the background fabric to make 36 triangle-squares from each for the blocks and border. Mark 3 squares 3⅜"x3⅜" on each of the print fabrics. Pair with the background fabric to make 6 triangle-squares from each for the blocks. Note: There will be some excess triangle-squares in both sizes.

From blue, green, aqua, and purple prints, cut 10 A each.
From pink, yellow, and apricot prints, cut 8 A each.
From each of the above prints, cut 1 strip 2½"x44" for the pieced binding.
From background print, cut 2 pieces 5½"x42" and 2 pieces 5½"x48".
From the remaining background, cut 32 B, 32 C, and 64 D.

Sewing
Sew and press as shown. Be sure to reverse half of the rectangle/triangle units. If Grid Triangle piecing was used, the A and B triangles are already sewn into squares. Make 5 blocks each from the blue, green, aqua, and purple prints and 4 blocks each from the pink, yellow, and apricot prints for a total of 32 blocks.

Make the top and bottom borders with 22 units in each. Make the side borders with 29 units in each.

Assembly
Place the blocks in a pleasing arrangement. Sew into diagonal rows, with the side and corner triangles at the ends.

Add the top and bottom triangle borders, then add the side triangle borders. Attach the print border and miter the corners.

Finishing
Quilt the blocks and background in a grid following the diagonal seams of the triangles. Mark and quilt the handprint in the borders, reversing the design to make both left and right hands. Sew and cut the pieced binding as described in the text. Bind to finish.

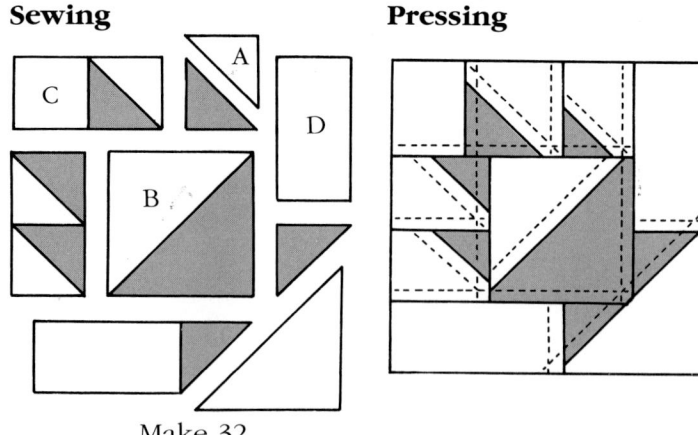

Make 32

Pat-a-Cake 49

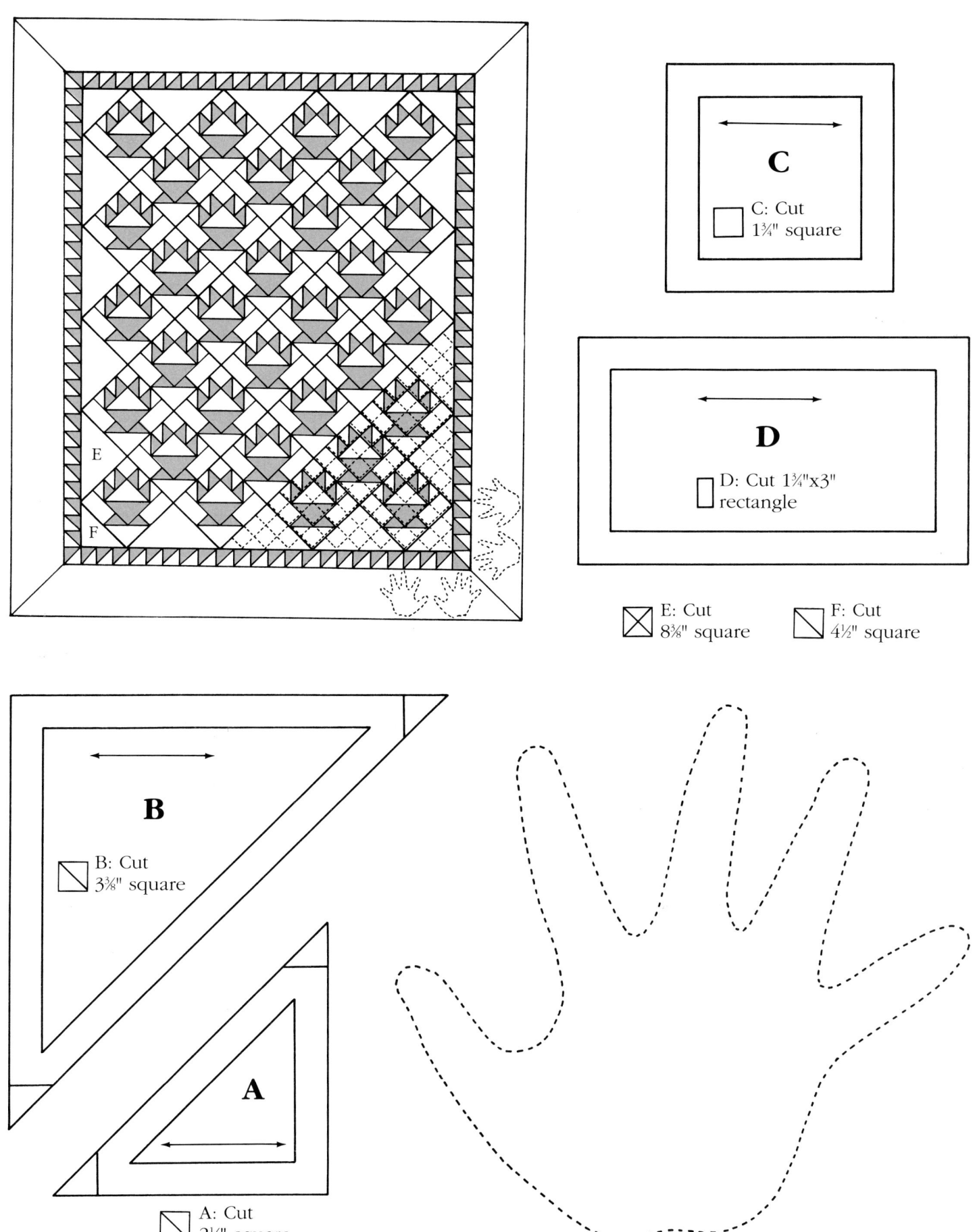

Daisy Chain

Daisies, both appliquéd and quilted, are scattered among the little flowered squares of the Nine Patch blocks in this variation of Single Irish Chain. Use a pretty print for the patchwork and match the appliqué colors to it. Although the squares are tiny (just one inch!), they're a breeze to make with strip piecing.

33"x45"   3" blocks
Shown in color on page 36.

Fabric Amounts
Nine Patch block and border (floral print) – 1½ yards
Background (cream) – 1¾ yards
Flowers (pink) – ¼ yard
Leaves (green) – ¼ yard
Flower centers and narrow border (blue) – ¼ yard
Backing – 1½ yards
Binding (blue) – ¾ yard

Cutting
From floral print, cut 2 pieces 3"x35", and 2 pieces 3"x47".
From remaining print, cut 26 strips 1½"x22".
From background fabric, cut 11 strips across the width of the fabric. Also from background, cut 41 A* and 18 B.
From green, cut 18 C.
From pink, cut 18 D.
From blue, cut cut 2 pieces 1"x29", 2 pieces 1"x41". Also from blue, cut 18 E.
*Tip: Wait to cut A until the Nine Patch blocks are made and measured.

Sewing
Sew the strips together in sets, as shown. Use 2 shorter print strips for 1 full-width strip. Make 5 side sets and 3 middle sets. Press the seams toward the print. Cut into 1½" sections. Make 58 Nine Patch blocks. Measure and cut A to match.

Crease the 18 larger background squares diagonally and into fourths. Center the leaf piece and appliqué the leaf portion only. Trim the center area. Appliqué the flower and center. Trim the block to 3½" or use pattern A.

Assembly
Following the photograph and diagram, arrange the blocks into 13 rows with 9 blocks in each. Sew together, pressing the seams toward the background squares.

Center and sew the blue and print border pieces together. Sew to the quilt and miter the corners.

Finishing
Quilt around the flowers. Quilt diagonal lines through the center of each Nine Patch block, extending the lines into the borders. Bind to finish.

Daisy Chain

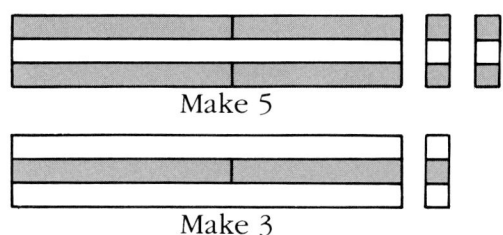
Make 5
Make 3

Sewing

Make 58

Pressing

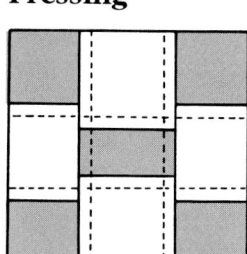

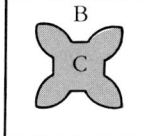 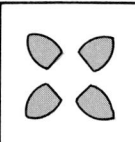  
Make 18

☐ B: Cut 5" square

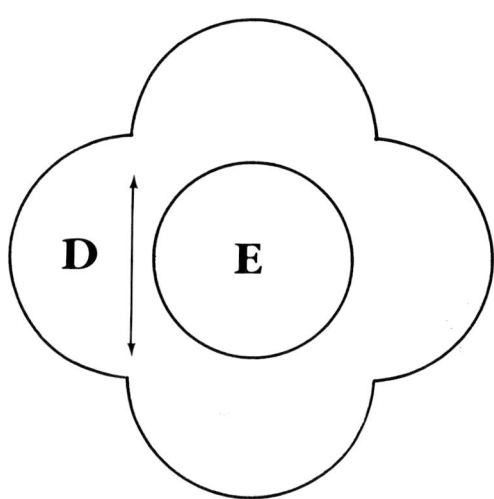

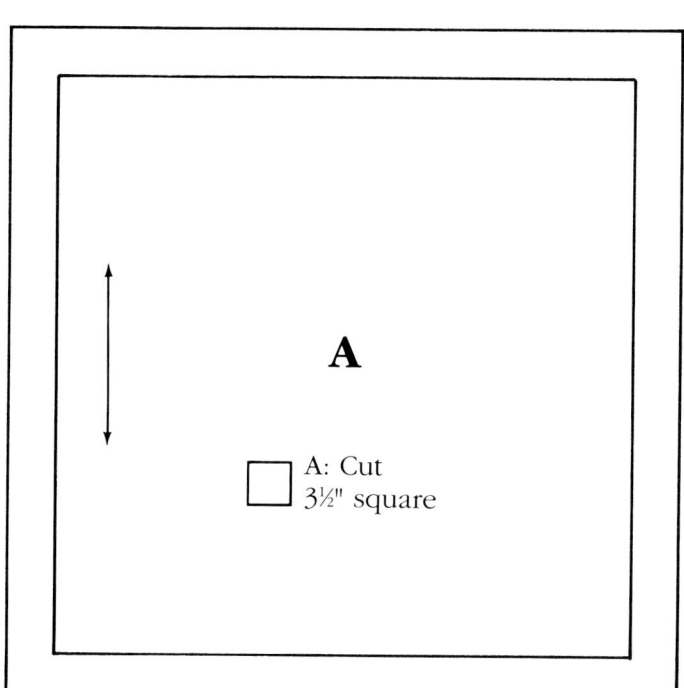

☐ A: Cut 3½" square

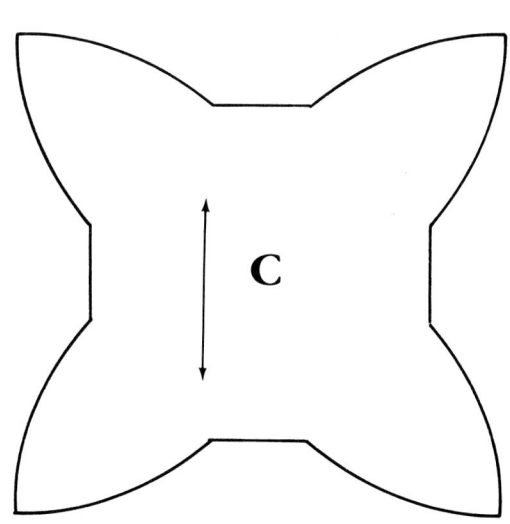

Little Gosling Chase

The Wild Goose Chase pattern becomes a framework for a gaggle of goslings. Add interest to the diagonal lines of the design by using two colors. Appliqué the geese then dress them up with silk ribbon bows.

38"x51"   6" blocks
Shown in color on page 36.

Fabric Amounts
Triangles (pink print, blue print) – 2 fabrics, ¾ yard each
Small triangles (cream print) – 1⅛ yards
Corner squares and triangles (multi-colored print) – ½ yard
Background (blue solid) – 1⅜ yards
Geese (cream) – ¾ yard
Beaks and feet (gold) – ⅛ yard
Backing – 1⅝ yards
Binding (multi-colored print) – ¾ yard
Bows (pink) – 5 yards 7mm wide silk ribbon

Cutting
From pink and blue prints, cut 96 A each.
From cream print, cut 384 B.
From multi-colored print, cut 17 C and 14 D.
From blue solid, cut 18 E, 10 F and 4 G.
From gold, cut 9 H, 9 Hr, 9 I and 9 Ir.
From cream, cut 9 J and 9 Jr.
Note: Patterns H, I and J are appliqué patterns.

Sewing
Sew as shown, joining the A and B triangles. Sew into groups of four. Make 24 blue groups and 24 pink groups.

Fold and crease the background squares diagonally. Match the reference mark on the geese pattern to the center of the creases. Appliqué the geese, inserting and appliquéing the feet and beaks as you sew. Using embroidery floss, make french knots for the eyes and a line of backstitches to outline the foremost foot. Make 18 geese blocks, with half facing the opposite direction. Trim the blocks to 6½" square.

Assembly
Following the photograph and diagram, arrange the triangle sections and appliqué blocks. Place the multi-colored squares and triangles between and at the ends of the blue and pink triangle sections. Sew into diagonal rows. Join the rows.

Finishing
Outline quilt the triangles and the appliquéd geese. Quilt a 1" grid in the background around the geese. Use a chenille needle to sew a 10" length of silk ribbon around the neck of each goose, sewing through the top layers only. Tie a bow and trim the ends. Bind to finish.

Little Gosling Chase

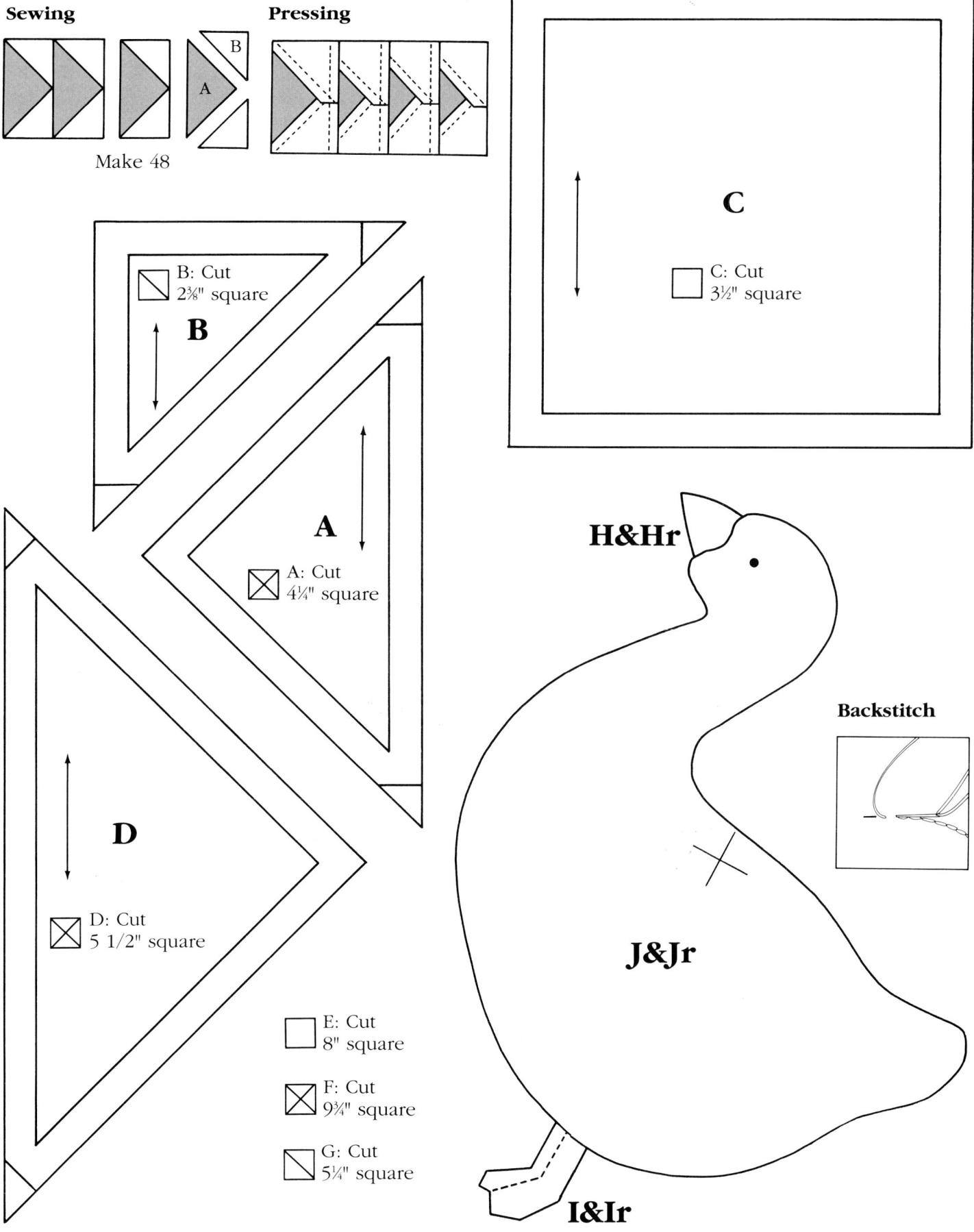

Sweet Hearts

The sweetest little hearts are made in candy colors. The scalloped swag border adds a touch of elegance. This is an excellent first appliqué project since the gentle curves are great for perfecting the appliqué stitch. Use bright primary colors for a fun variation.

30"x35" 4½" blocks
Shown in color on page 37.

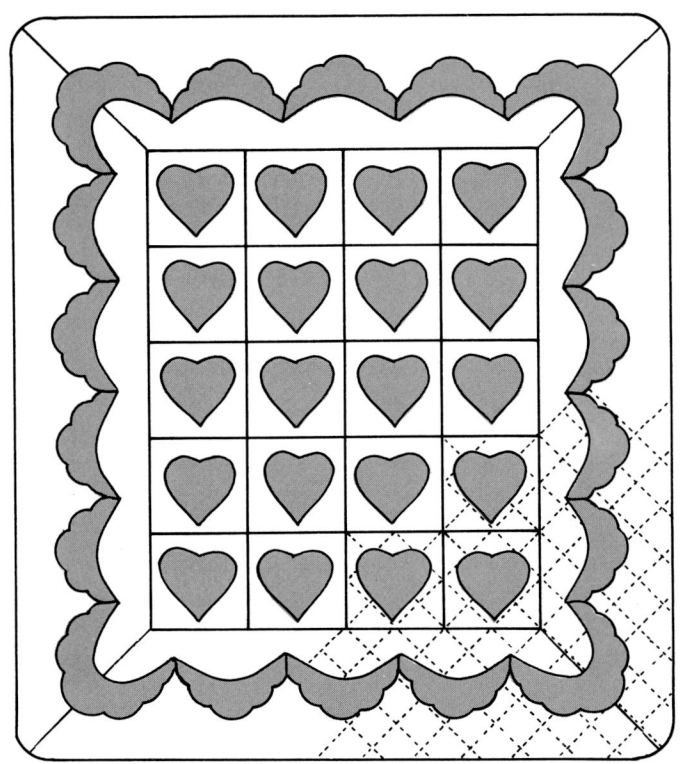

Fabric Amounts
Hearts (yellow, pink, lavender, aqua, blue, and periwinkle solids) – 6 fabrics, ¼ yard each
Background (white) – 1½ yards
Backing – 1¼ yards
Binding (multi-colored print) – ¾ yard

Cutting
From background, cut 2 pieces 7"x32", and 2 pieces 7"x37".
From remaining background, cut 20 A.
From 6 solids, cut a total of 20 B, 14 C, and 4 D.
Note: B, C, and D are appliqué patterns.

Sewing
Lightly crease the squares into fourths. Position the hearts, using the guidelines on the pattern. Appliqué, using needle-turn or paper-baste techniques. After the appliqué is complete, trim the squares to 5". Make 20 blocks.

Crease the border pieces 2 inches from one long edge. Mark the placement of the swags every 5¼ inches. Begin in the center for the side borders, and on either side of the center for the top and bottom borders. Appliqué the swags between the marks. Trim the border to 6½" wide after the swags are sewn.

Assembly
Sew the blocks into 5 rows with 4 blocks in each. Sew the borders, mitering the corners. Appliqué the four corner swags. Use the pattern to mark the rounded corners but wait to trim the fabric until the quilting is complete.

Finishing
Quilt around each heart and swag. Quilt the background in a diagonal grid. Cut 2" bias strips for the binding. Bind to finish.

Sewing

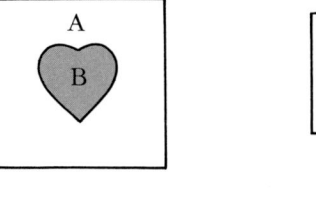

Make 20

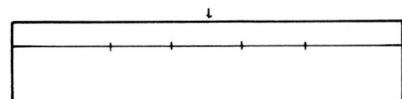

Top and bottom borders

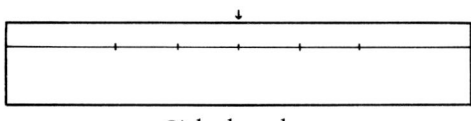

Side borders

Sweet Hearts 55

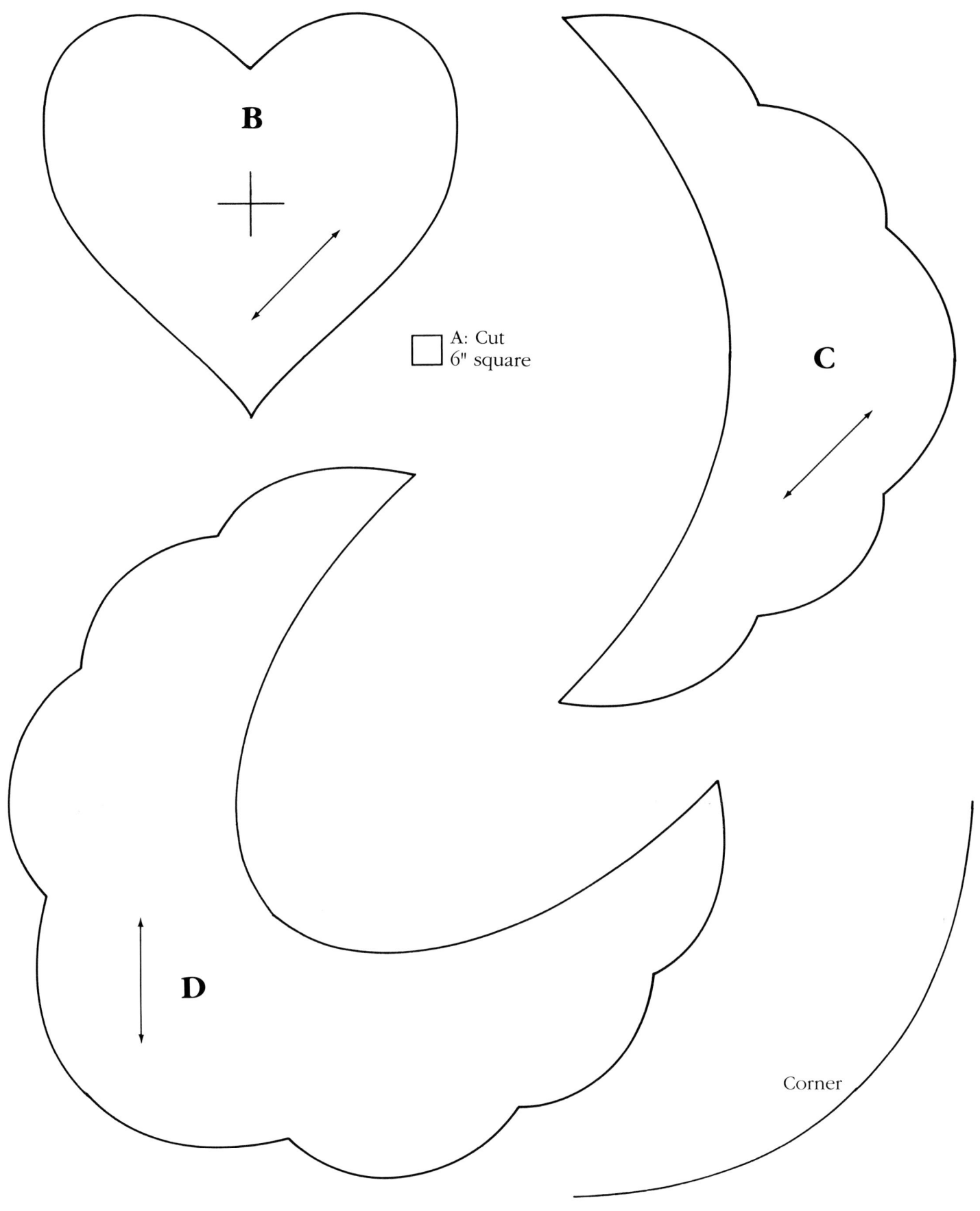

Ribbon Twist

Like so many tangled ribbons, lots of pretty prints are used in this fascinating design. Just two easy blocks create the interwoven pattern. The angled edges add to the charm!

33"x40"   3¾" blocks
Shown in color on page 37.

Fabric Amounts
Background (pink print) – 1 yard
Ribbons (pink, apricot, blue, green, yellow, and purple prints) – 3 fabrics in each of 6 colors, ⅛ each
Backing – 1⅓ yards

Cutting
From background, cut 50 A and 49 B.
From each of 18 prints, cut 13 B, 13 C and 2 D.
From each of 4 prints, cut an additional 1 D.

Sewing
Before sewing, arrange the pieces into the design. Place two or three rows at a time. Each fabric should be used once along the edge and the 4 fabrics with 3 of the D pieces should be used for the corners. Sew the blocks first, then make the partial blocks on the edges.

Sew the A blocks as shown, first creasing or marking the diagonal seam on the small squares. Press, then trim the seam to ¼". Make 50 blocks.

Make the B blocks as shown, beginning with a partial seam. Open the piece, with the seam allowance away from the center, and add the next rectangle. Continue adding the pieces in order, always keeping the seams away from the center. Finish the partial seam. Make 49 blocks.

Sew the partial blocks, keeping them separate from the blocks. Make 14 for the sides and 4 for the corners. There will be some excess B and C pieces.

Assembly
Alternate the placement of the blocks, beginning and ending each row with the A block. Make 11 rows, with 9 blocks in each.
Add the partial blocks, stitching only on the sewing line and backstitching.

Finishing
Outline quilt the blocks, then quilt the bow design. Wait to quilt the edges until the edges have been clean-finished as described in the text.

Sewing

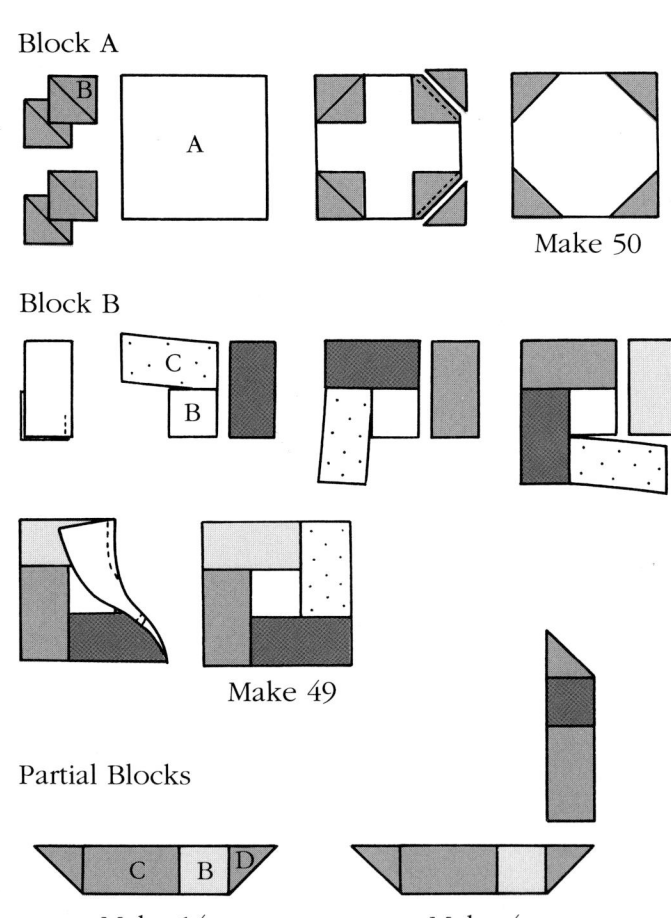

Block A

Make 50

Block B

Make 49

Partial Blocks

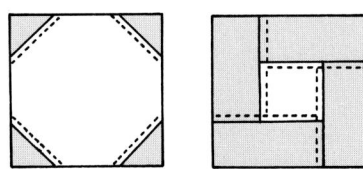

Make 14   Make 4

Pressing

Ribbon Twist

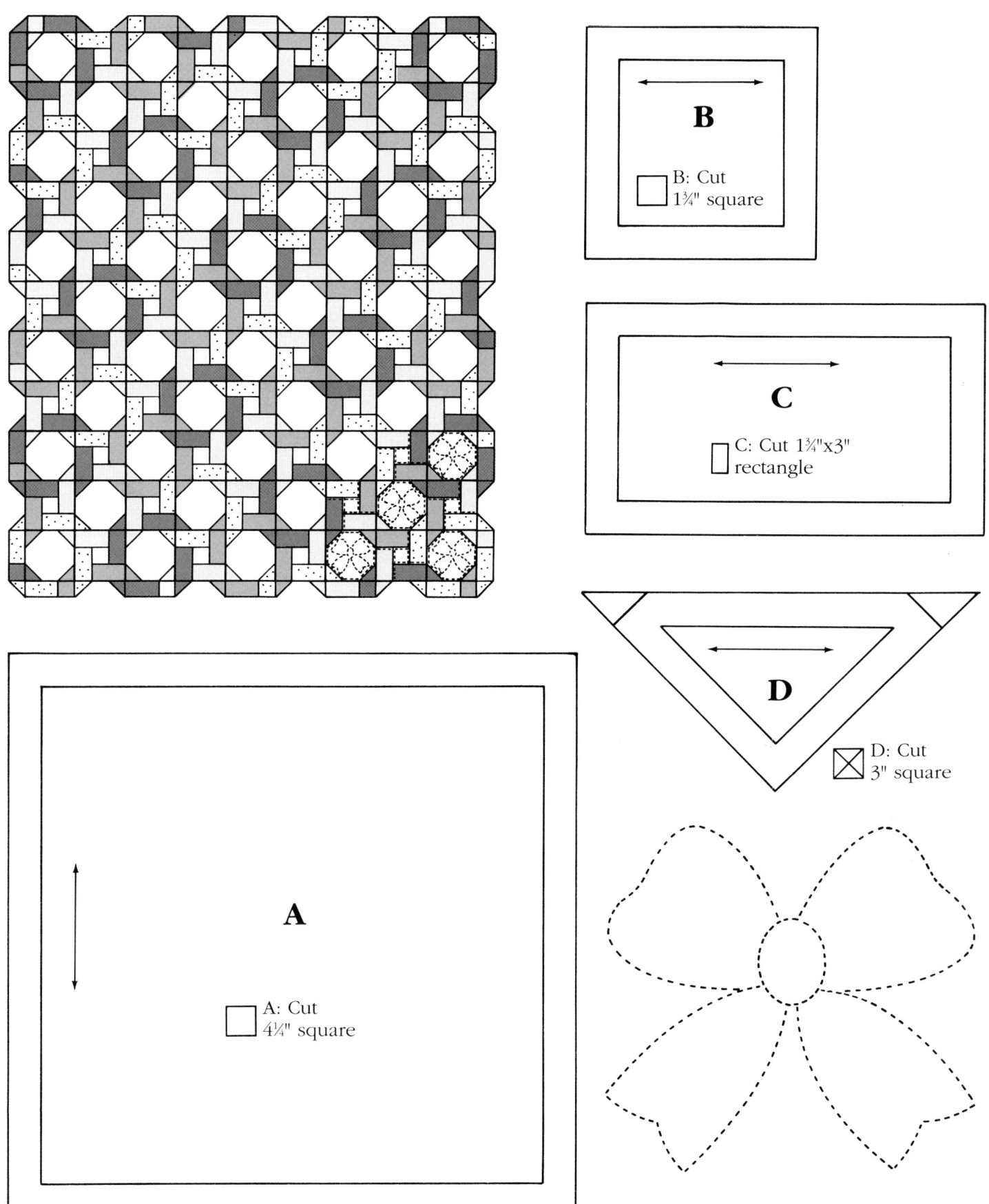

B: Cut 1¾" square

C: Cut 1¾"x3" rectangle

D: Cut 3" square

A: Cut 4¼" square

Twinkle, Twinkle

Like diamonds in the sky, these little patchwork stars sparkle! Use lots of clear pastels or find five perfect prints for the stars. An original design, this quilt is best made with hand piecing and continuous hand piecing techniques.

39"x54" 4½" blocks
Shown in color on page 38.

Fabric Amounts
Star points (yellow, pink, purple, blue, apricot and green) – 3 prints in each of 6 colors, ⅛ yard each
Background (white) – 1¾ yards
Alternate blocks (medium blue print) – 1 yard
Border (bright blue print) – 1⅜ yards
Backing – 1¾ yards
Binding (bright blue print) – ¾ yard

Cutting
From 18 prints, cut a total of 175 A (approximately 10 from each) for blocks. Also from the prints, cut a total of 146 A (approximately 8 from each) and 4 K for borders.
From white background, cut 35 B, 35 Br, 35 C, 35 Cr, and 35 D for blocks. Also from background, cut 142 H, 4 I, 4 Ir, 142 J, 4 L and 4 Lr for borders.
From medium blue, cut 24 E, 20 F, and 4 G.
From bright blue, cut 4 M. Also cut 2 pieces 1½"x34" and 2 pieces 1½"x47" for inner borders. Cut 2 pieces 1½"x41" and 2 pieces 1½"x 56" for outer borders. Note: Cut the blue borders after the patchwork border is completed. The width and length can be adjusted, if necessary.

Sewing
Sew and press the blocks as shown. Use continuous hand piecing, as described in the text, to add the background pieces with one continuous seam. Make 35 blocks.

Sew and press the borders as shown, using continuous hand piecing to first add the larger background triangles, then the smaller triangles, to the points. Add the small I triangle at the ends. Make 2 sections with 31 points and 2 with 42 points. Add the corner points and triangles to the longer sections.

Assembly
Sew in diagonal rows, alternating the blocks with the blue squares and ending each row with the blue triangles. Measure the quilt top and the border sections and adjust the width of the bright blue border, if necessary. Add the blue border, mitering the corners. Add the patchwork border and sew the corner seams. Add the outer blue border, with the small M piece at each corner.

Finishing
Outline the points in the stars and border with quilting. Quilt the star design in the alternate squares. Bind to finish.

Twinkle, Twinkle

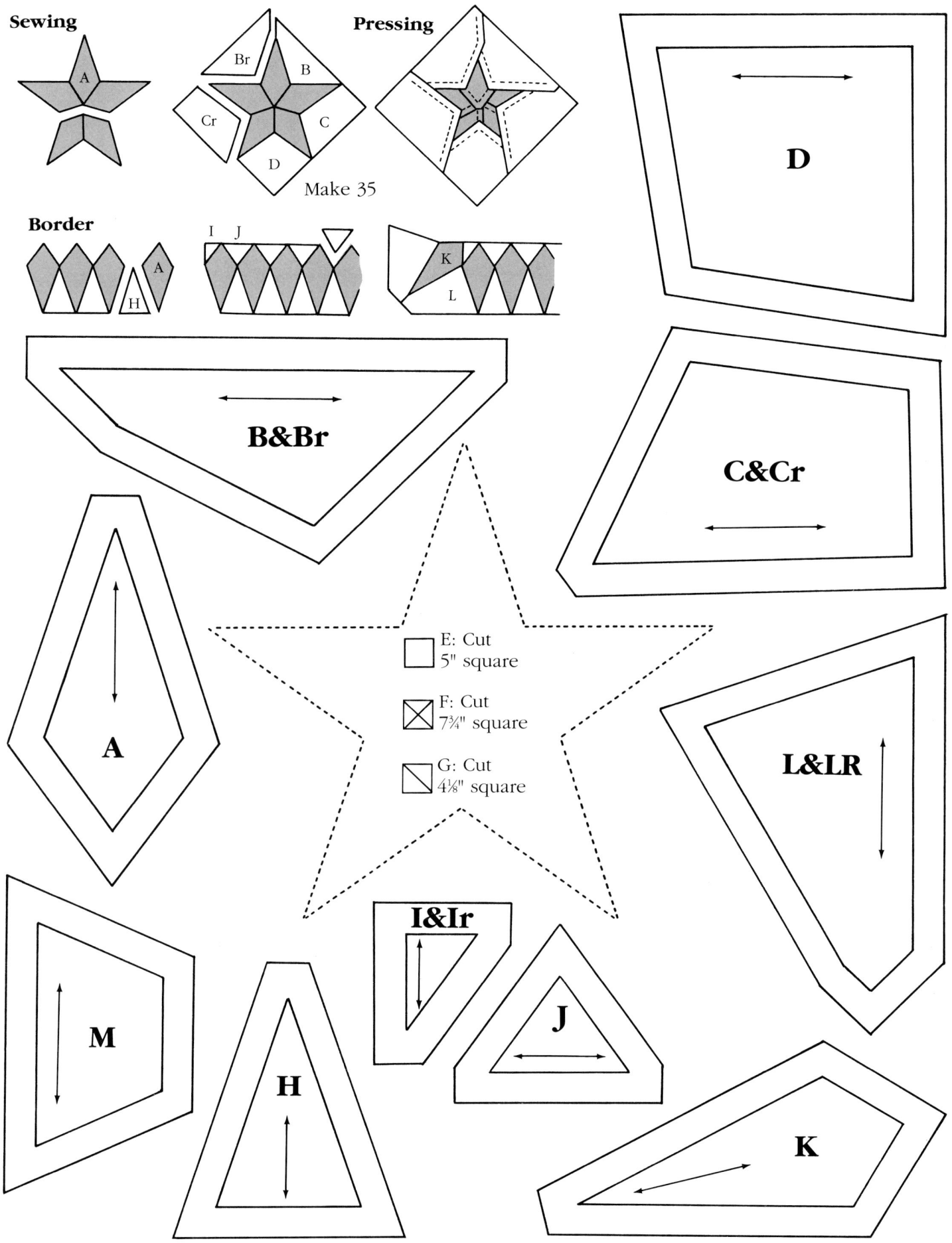

Bright Hopes

Babies bring the brightest of hopes to us all. Share the joy with this delightfully easy quilt. Use four different colors to make the best of the woven effect. Prairie points in the little starry print add a sparkling finish.

33"x39" 5½" blocks
Shown in color on page 38.

Fabric Amounts
Center (white print) – ⅜ yard
Rectangles (bright blue, pink, yellow, green prints) –
   4 fabrics, ½ yard each
Backing – 1⅓ yards
Prairie points (white print) – 1 yard

Cutting
From white print, cut 42 A. Also from white print,
   cut 70 C for prairie point edging.
From bright prints, cut 42 B each.

Sewing
Sew as shown, beginning with a partial seam. Place a rectangle on a center square, sewing from the middle to the edge. Open the piece and add the next rectangle. Keep the seam away from the center. Add two more rectangles, again with their seams away from the center. Finish the sewing on the first seam. The colors should be added in the same order on all the blocks. Make 42 blocks. Tip: Do the partial seam on all the blocks then use chain piecing to add the next three rectangles to all the blocks.

Assembly
Make 7 rows with 6 blocks in each. Keep the colors in the same positions throughout the rows.

Finishing
Quilt the star design and next to the seams. Make and attach the prairie points as described in the text, using 16 for the top and bottom and 19 for the sides. Finish the quilting at the edges.

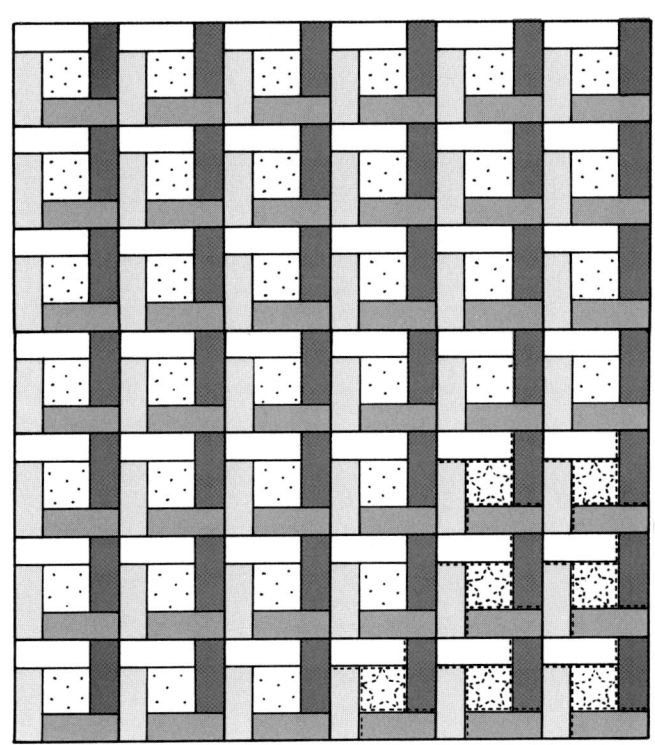

Sewing

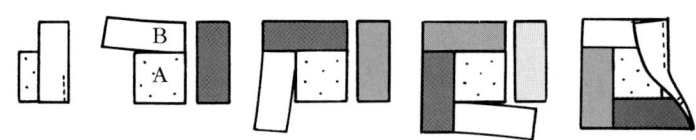

Pressing

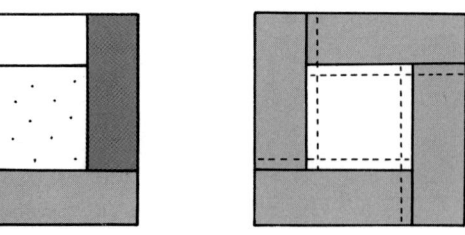

Make 42

Bright Hopes

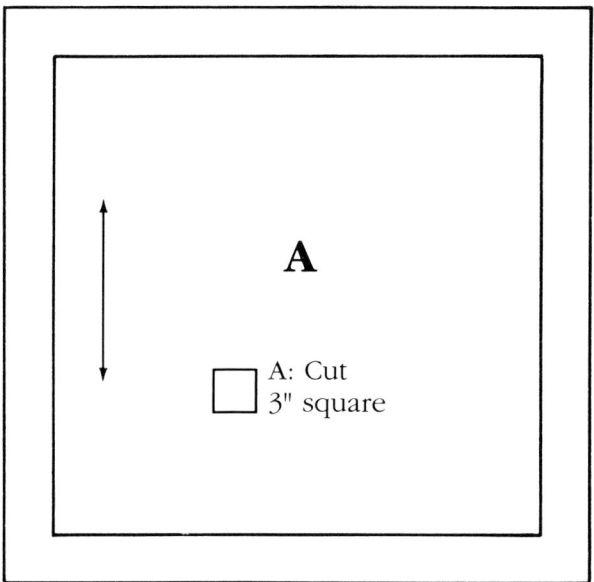
A: Cut 3" square

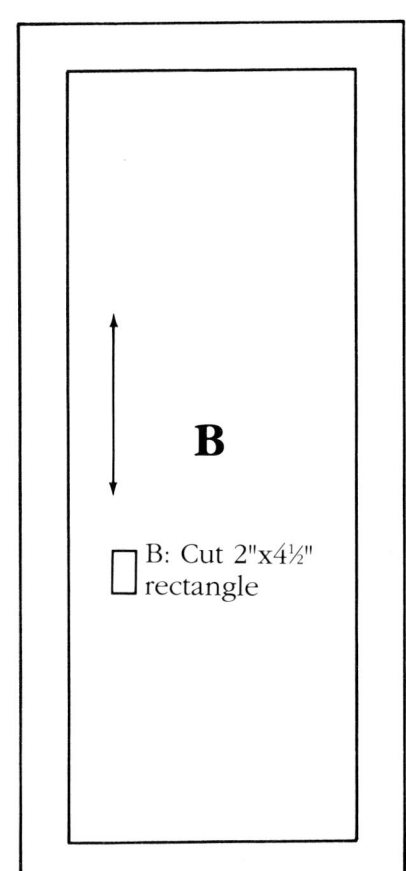
B: Cut 2"x4½" rectangle

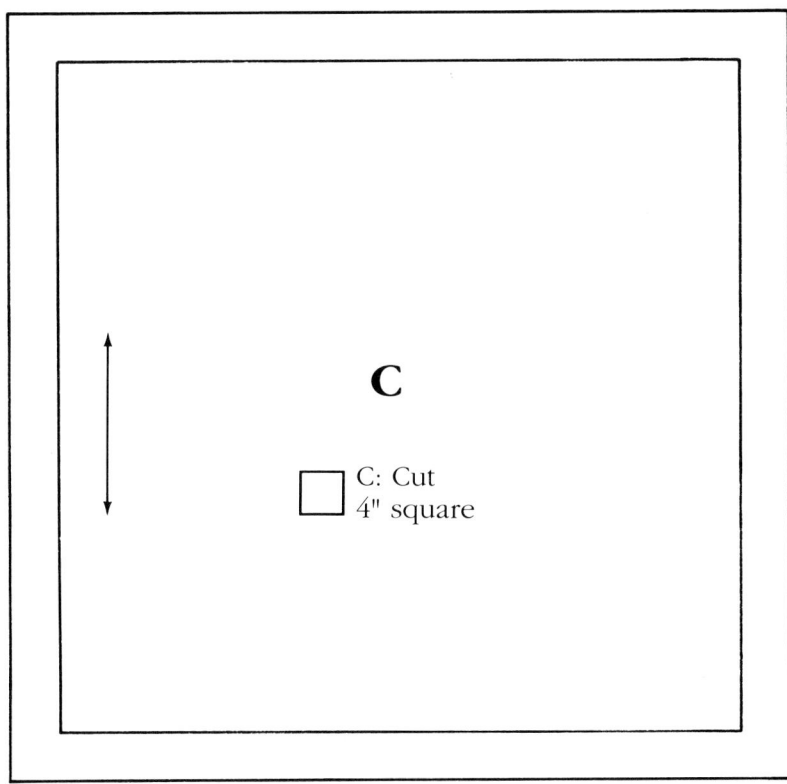
C: Cut 4" square

Duck and Ducklings

The traditional Duck and Ducklings design is brought to life in cheery plaids while Mama Duck proudly parades her babies around the border. A terrific secondary design emerges when the blocks are set side by side.

41"x49" 7½" blocks
Shown in color on page 39.

Fabric Amounts
Triangles and ducks (plaids) – 10 fabrics, ¼ yard each
Background (white) – 2¼ yards
Beaks (gold) – ⅛ yard
Narrow borders (blue solid) – 1½ yards
Backing – 3 yards (2 lengths)
Binding – ¾ yard (or use excess from blue solid)

Cutting
From plaids, cut 8 A, 8 B, and 2 D each. Also from plaid fabrics, cut a total of 4 E, 10 F, and 4 G.
From white background, cut 2 pieces 6"x43" and 2 pieces 6"x51".
From remaining background, cut 240 A and 80 C.
From gold fabric, cut 4 Beak E, 10 Beak F, and 4 Beak G.
From the blue solid, cut 2 pieces 1½"x32" and 2 pieces 1½"x40".
Note: Patterns E, F, and G are appliqué patterns.

Sewing
Sew and press as shown. Make 20 blocks, 2 from each plaid.

Arrange the ducks on the border and make a small mark for placement. Appliqué the ducks, inserting and appliquéing the beaks as you sew. Don't sew the bottom edges of the ducks; let them extend into the seam of the blue border. Make french knots using embroidery floss for the eyes. After the appliqué is complete, trim the borders to 5" wide.

Assembly
Place the blocks in a pleasing arrangement. Sew into 5 rows with 4 blocks in each.

Center and sew the blue borders to the appliquéd borders, pressing the seams toward the blue. Sew the borders to the quilt, mitering the corners.

Finishing
Outline quilt the blocks and around the ducks. Quilt the border in diagonal lines that extend in a 45 degree angle from the seams in the blocks. Bind to finish.

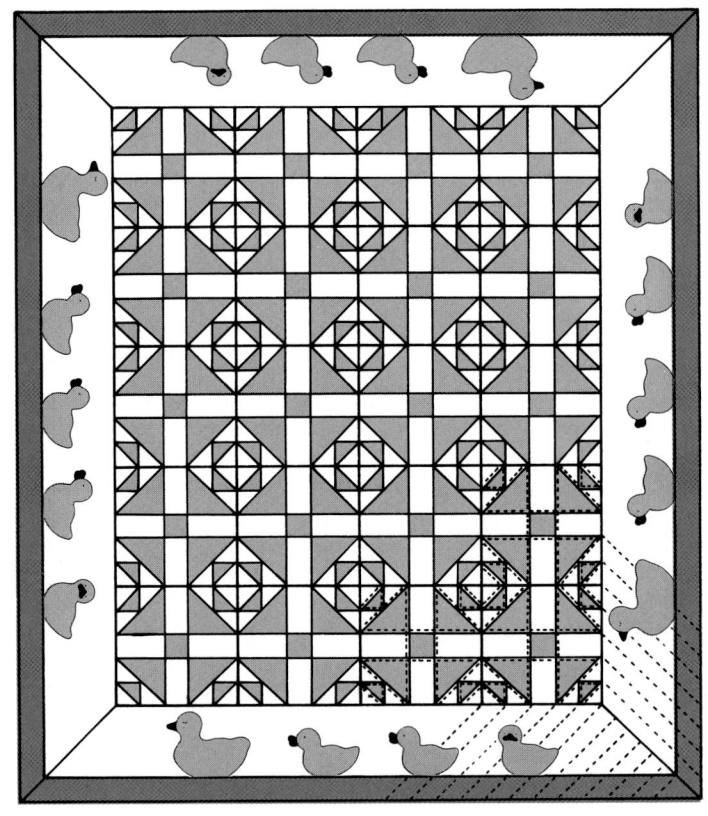

Sewing

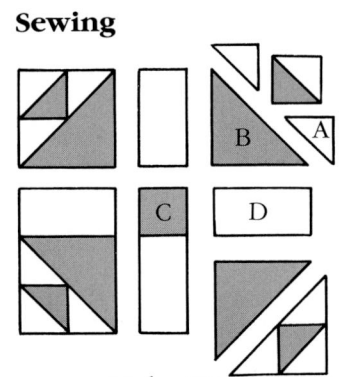

Pressing

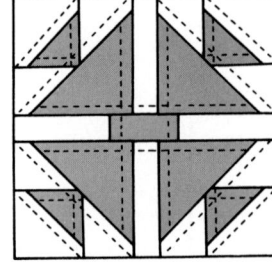

Make 20

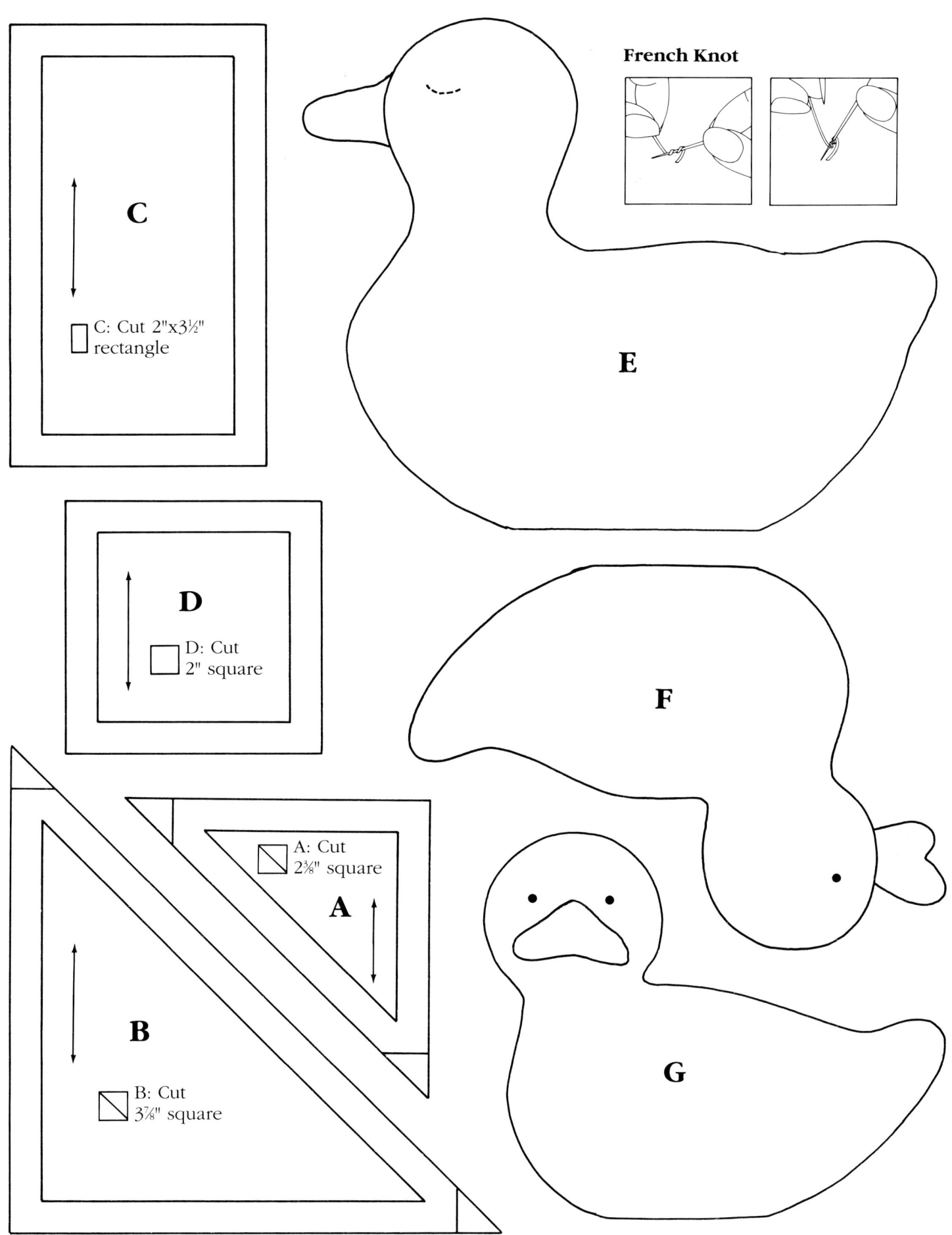

Baby Bunting

"Bye Baby Bunting, Daddy's gone a-hunting, for a little rabbit skin, to wrap his little baby in", but this quilt is much prettier! The old, yet seldom seen, Baby Bunting pattern is perfect in pastels. Add meaning, and a lot of fun, by quilting the little hopping bunnies all around.

36"x48"   6" blocks
Shown in color on page 39.

Fabric Amounts
Points (white) – ¾ yard
Background of points (blue, turquoise, yellow, and apricot solids) – 4 fabrics, ¼ yard each
Background of points (green and pink solids) – 2 fabrics, ⅓ yard each
Curved shapes (blue, turquoise, yellow, and apricot prints) – 4 fabrics, ⅓ yard each
Curved shapes (green, pink, and lavender prints) – ¾ yard each
Backing – 1⅝ yards
Binding (lavender print) – ¾ yard

Cutting
From white, cut 288 B.
From blue and turquoise solids, cut 4 A, 4 Ar, and 20 C each.
From yellow and apricot solids, cut 8 A, 8 Ar, and 40 C each.
From green and pink solids, cut 12 A, 12 Ar, and 60 C each.
From blue and turquoise prints, cut 4 E each.
From yellow and apricot prints, cut 12 D each.
From green print, cut 4 D and 16 E.
From pink print, cut 20 D and 4 E.
From lavender print, cut 20 E.

Sewing
For best results, use hand piecing techniques. Sew and press as shown, using continuous sewing on the points. Match the marks on the curved shapes (D and E) to the seams of the pieced arc.

Make the following number of blocks in these combinations, for a total of 48 blocks:

Make 4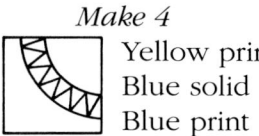
Yellow print
Blue solid
Blue print

Make 8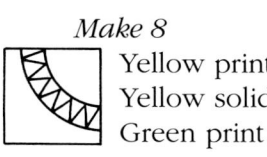
Yellow print
Yellow solid
Green print

Make 4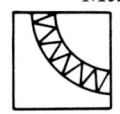
Green print
Green solid
Pink print

Make 8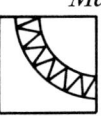
Pink print
Green solid
Green print

Make 8
Apricot print
Apricot solid
Lavender print

Make 4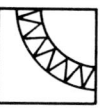
Apricot print
Turquoise solid
Turquoise print

Make 12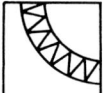
Pink print
Pink solid
Lavender print

Baby Bunting

Assembly
Arrange the blocks according to the photograph and diagram. Make 8 rows, with 6 blocks in each.

Finishing
Outline the points in each block with quilting. Quilt the bunny designs in the curved shapes, reversing where necessary. Bind to finish.

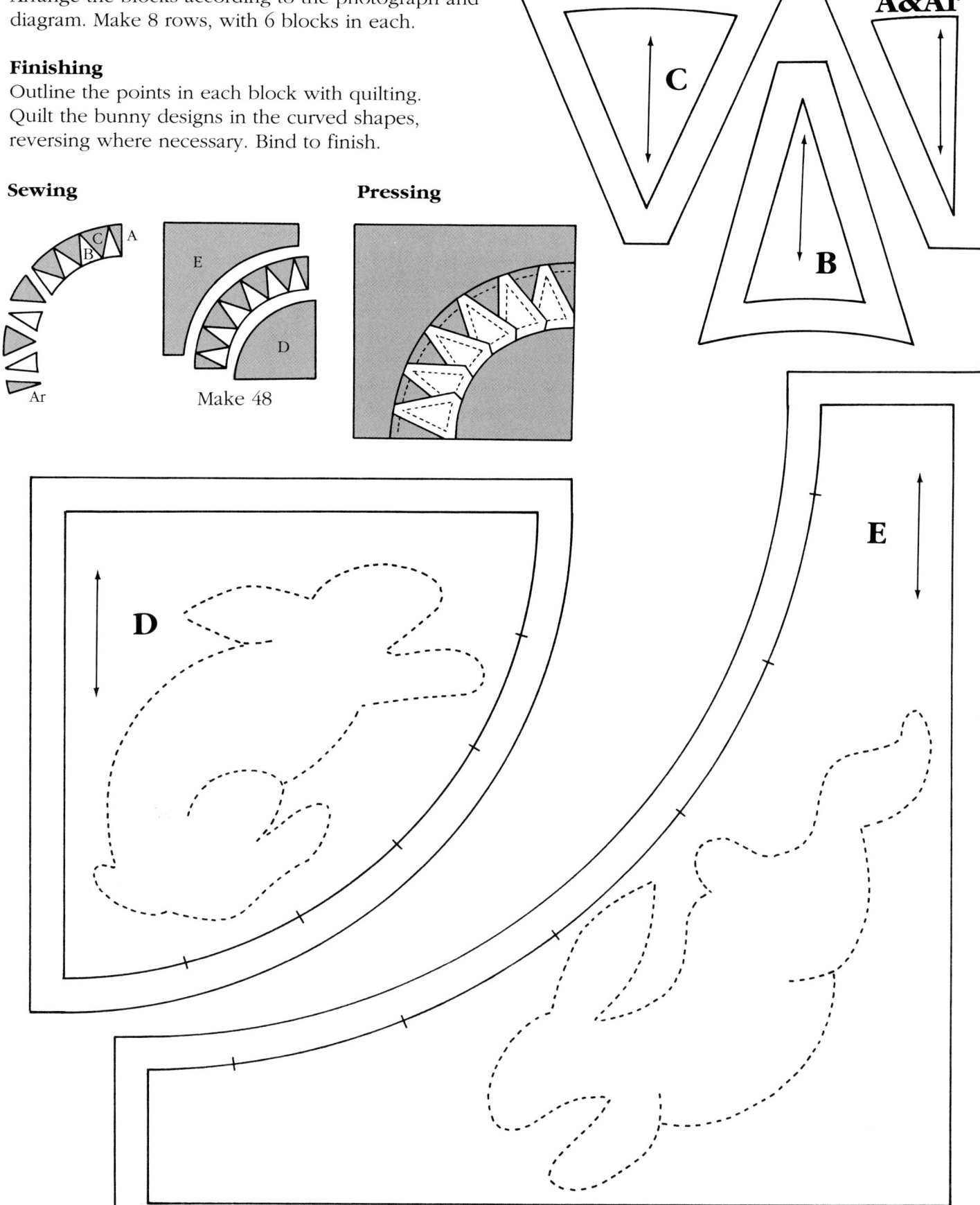

Make 48

Whiligig

Looking like a puff of wind could start them twirling, these blocks each use two prints, with one slightly darker. The background print forms another pinwheel in the corners of the blocks. Prairie points in all the colors add to the fun!

36"x48"   6" blocks
Shown in color on page 40.

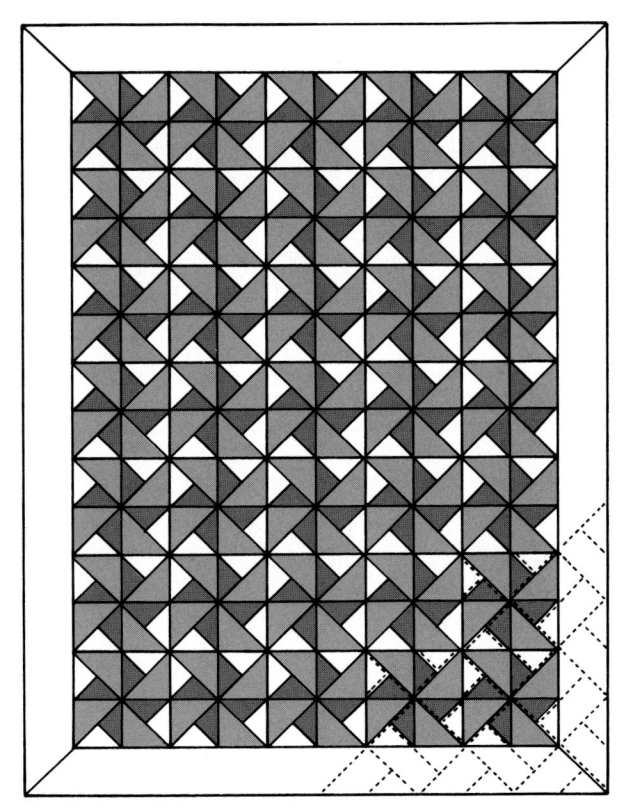

Fabric Amounts
Small triangles (two navys, two wines, one gold, one dark green) – 6 fabrics, ⅜ yard each
Large triangles (two blues, two pinks, one yellow, one green) – 6 fabrics, ⅜ yard each
Background (cream print) – 1⅝ yards
Prairie points – Included in above amounts or ⅛ yard of 12 fabrics if purchased separately.
Backing – 1⅝ yards

Cutting
From navy, wine, and dark green fabrics, cut 24 A each.
From gold print, cut 20 A.
From blue, pink, and green fabrics, cut 24 B each.
From yellow fabric, cut 20 B.
From the above prints, cut a total of 78 C (approximately 7 from each) for prairie point edging.
From cream background, cut 2 pieces 3½"x38" and 2 pieces 3½"x50".
From the remaining background, cut 140 A.

Sewing
Sew and press the blocks as shown. Make 6 blocks each from the navy, wine, and green combinations and 5 blocks from the gold combination for a total of 35 blocks.

Assembly
Place the blocks in a pleasing arrangement. Make 7 rows, with 5 blocks in each. Add the border pieces, mitering the corners.

Finishing
Quilt next to the diagonal seams. Attach the prairie points as described in the text, using 18 for the top and bottom and 21 for each of the sides. Finish the quilting by extending the quilting lines into the border.

Sewing

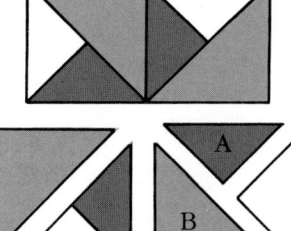

Pressing

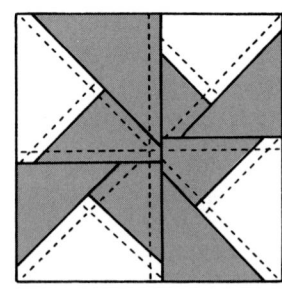

Make 35

Whiligig

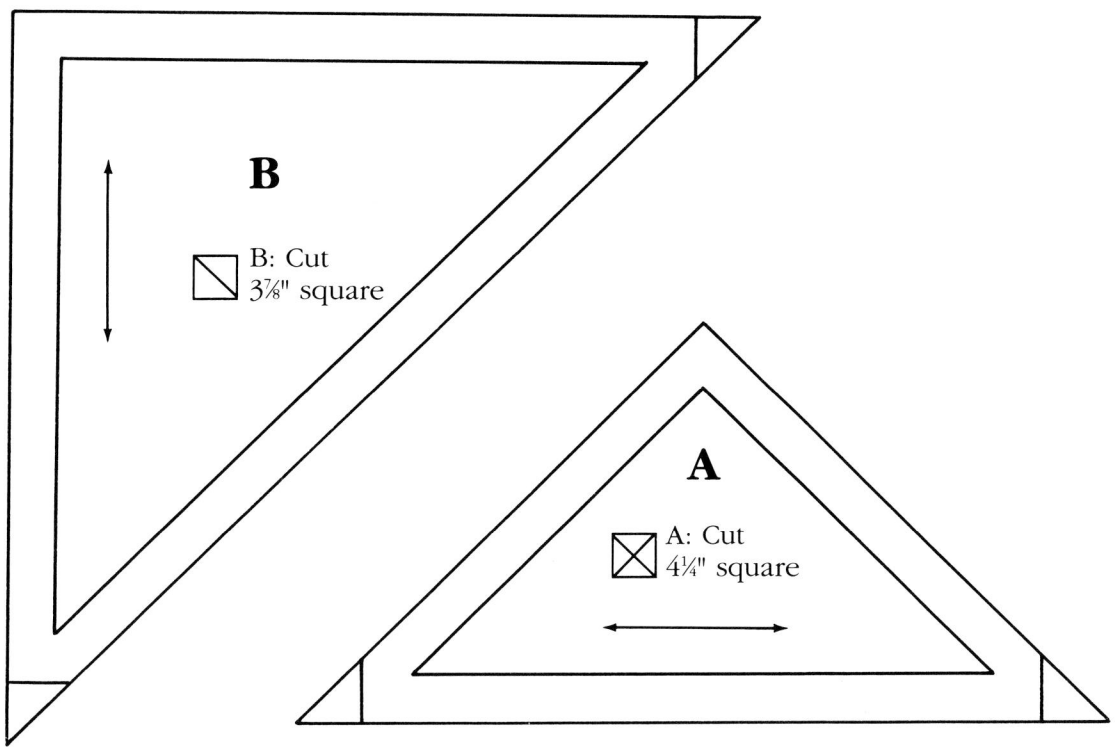
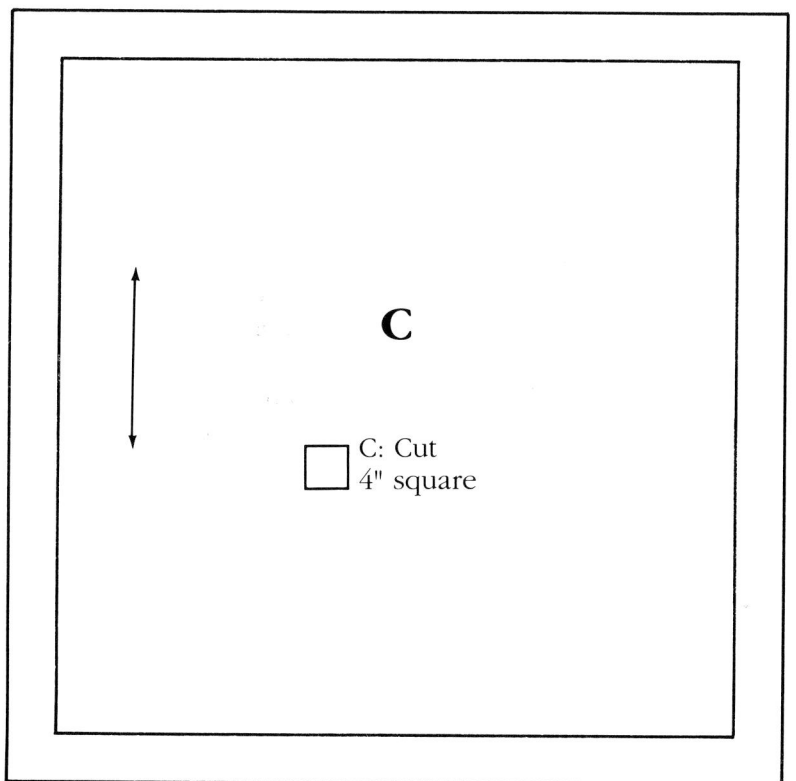

Railroad Crossing

Calico trains choo-choo along a patchwork track in this cheery version of a traditional pattern. Each rectangle represents a railroad tie and quilting forms the metal tracks. Some bright prints and lots of quilting make this quilt a wonderful gift for the special little boy in your life.

39"x50"
Shown in color on page 40.

Fabric Amounts
Patchwork (assorted prints) – 8 fabrics, ¼ yard each
Background (light print) – 2¼ yards
Corner squares (blue print) – ⅓ yard
Train (blue for engine, green for passenger car, brown for coal car, turquoise for freight car, red for caboose) – 5 fabrics, ¼ yard each
Train details (light gray for smoke, dark gray for coal, brown for logs, dark blue for freight door) – 4 fabrics, ⅛ yard each
Wheels, couplings and coal car (black chintz) – ½ yard
Backing – 1⅝ yards
Binding (blue print) – ¾ yard

Cutting
From 8 prints, cut a total of 144 A and 134 Z (approximately 18 A and 17 Z from each) or rotary cut 3 strips 1½"x44" from each for strip piecing.
From background, cut 2 pieces 1¼"x27" and 2 pieces 1¼"x38" for inner borders. Cut 2 pieces 7"x41" and 2 pieces 7"x52" for outer borders.
From remaining background, cut 8 B, 6 C, and 4 D.
From blue print, cut 7 E and 10 F.
From the train and detail fabrics, cut 4 engines (G, H, I, J), 4 coal cars (K, L), 4 passenger cars (O), 4 cabooses (P), 2 freight cars (M, N), and 2 lumber cars (R, S).
From the black, cut 2 Q, 40 T, 4 U, 4 V, 6 W, 4 X, and 16 Y.
Note: The patterns from G to Y are appliqué patterns.

Sewing
Template piecing – Sew the rectangles (A) into groups of 6, to make 24 sections. Make the patchwork border by sewing the small squares (Z) into 2 rows of 26 squares each and 2 rows of 41 squares each.

Strip piecing – Sew the 24 cut strips into sets of 6, each with a different order of fabrics. Press the seams in each of the 4 sets to one side. Cut 3½" wide sections, 6 from each set, for a total of 24 sections.

Make the patchwork border by cutting 6 sections 1½" wide from each set for a total of 24 sections. Join 5 sections end to end for each of the top and bottom borders, removing 4 squares to make rows of 26 squares. Join 7 sections end to end for each of the side borders, removing 1 square to make rows of 41 squares.

Crease the wide border pieces 1¼" from the long edges. Appliqué the trains, placing the bottom of each car on the crease so the wheels will touch the patchwork border. The trains are centered in each border. After the appliqué is completed, trim the borders to 6" wide.

Assembly
Sew the strip sections, setting squares, and background squares and triangles into diagonal rows. Add the inner borders and miter the corners. Add the patchwork border to the top and bottom, then the sides. Add the appliqué border, mitering the corners.

Finishing
Mark and quilt the small train design in the background squares. Quilt the strip sections with 2 lines of stitching ¾" from each edge. Outline the appliqué with quilting. Quilt a diagonal grid every ¾", with the lines connecting with the 1" squares in the border. Bind to finish.

Railroad Crossing

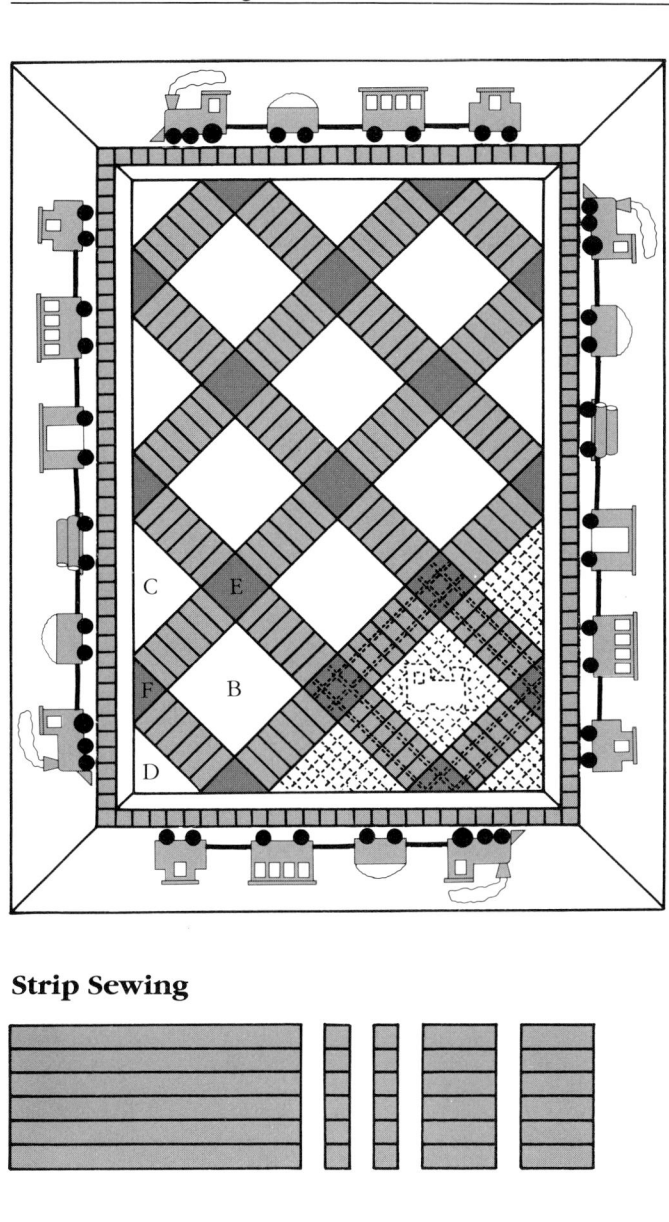

Strip Sewing

Template Sewing   **Pressing**

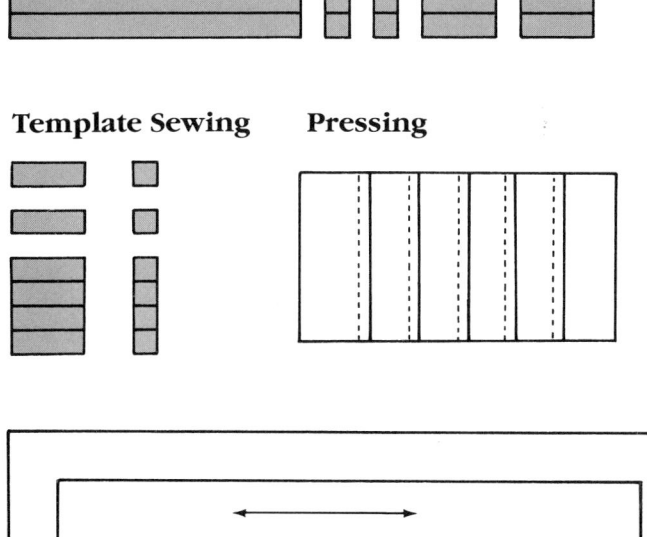

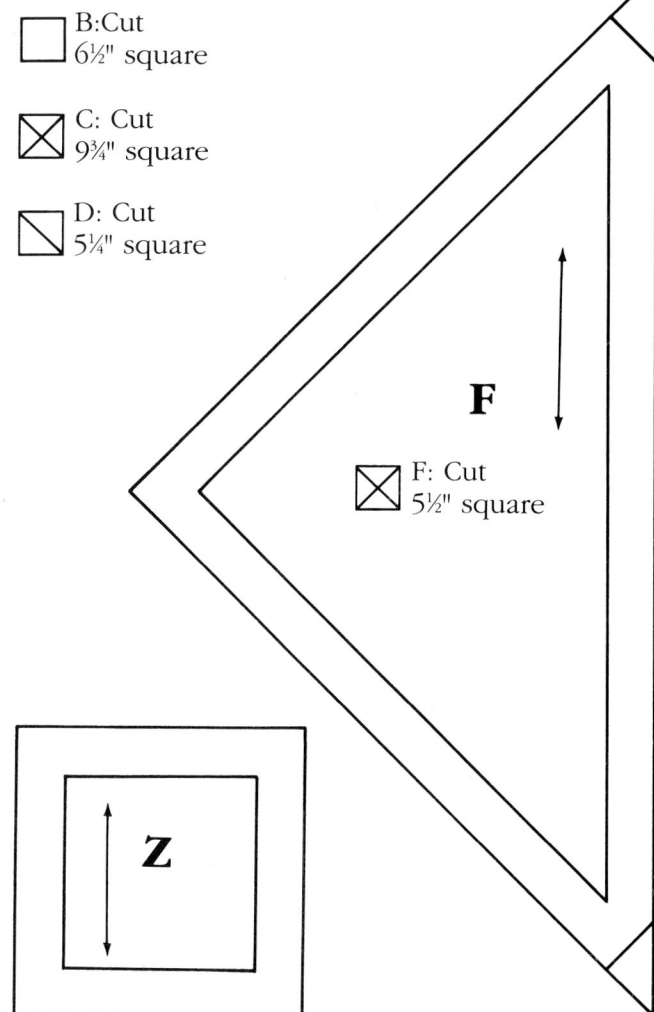

B: Cut 6½" square

C: Cut 9¾" square

D: Cut 5¼" square

F: Cut 5½" square

Z

E

E: Cut 3½" square

A

A: Cut 1½"x3½" rectangle

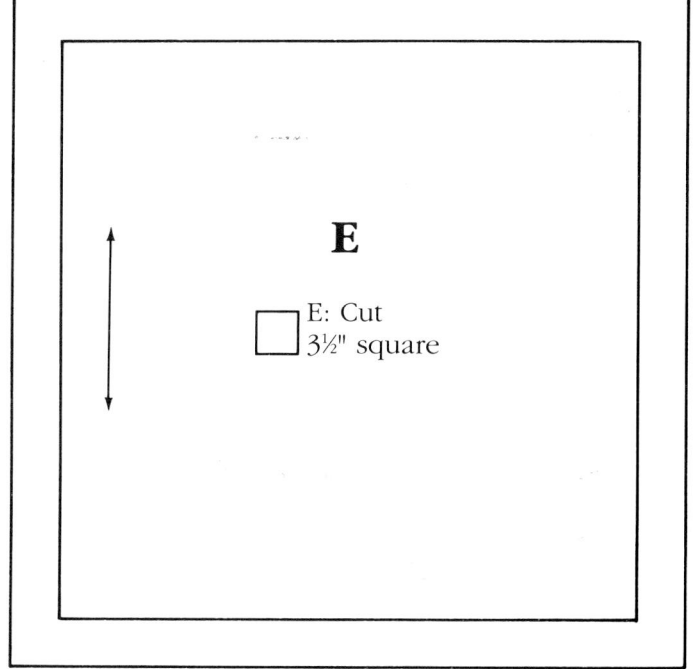

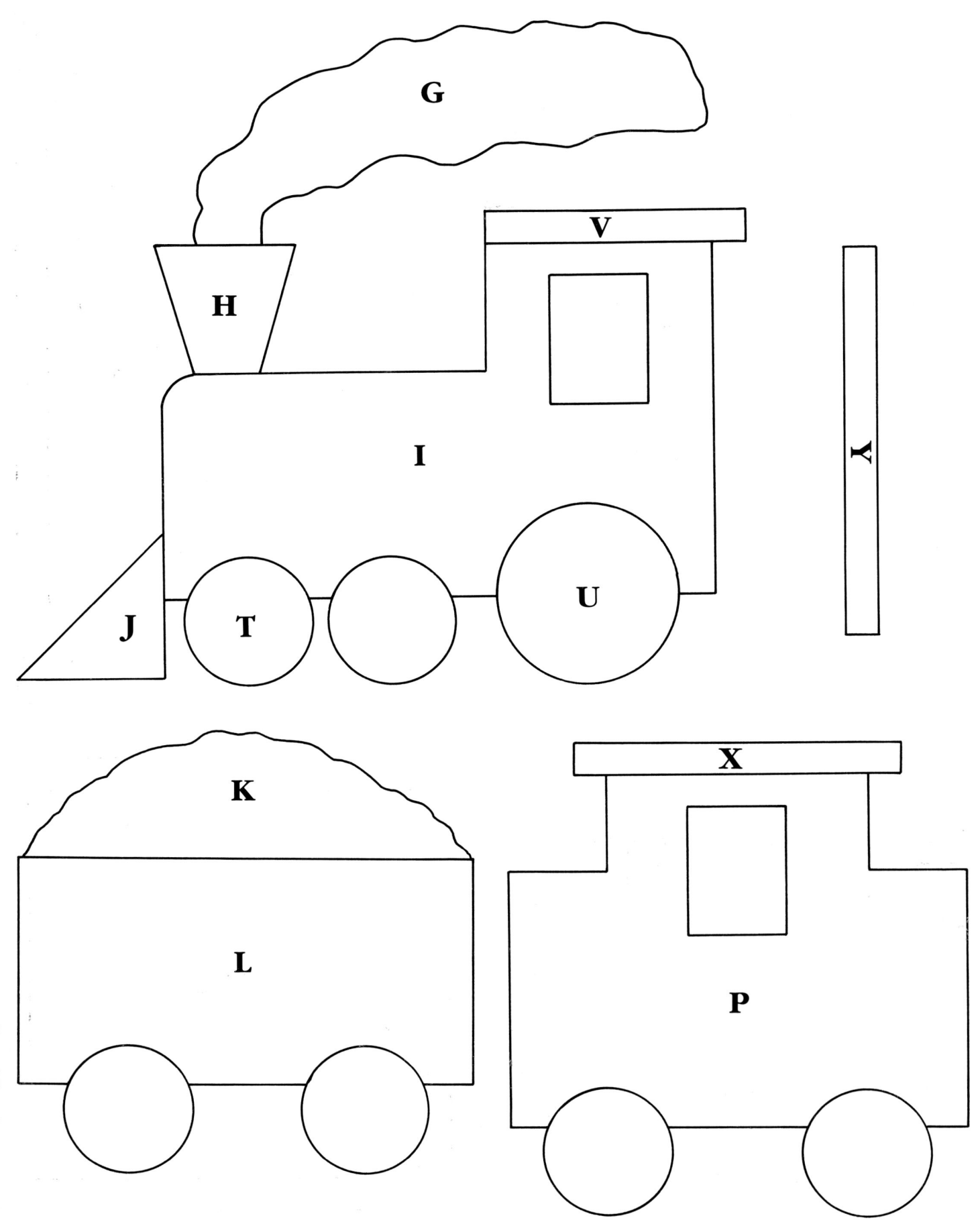

Railroad Crossing

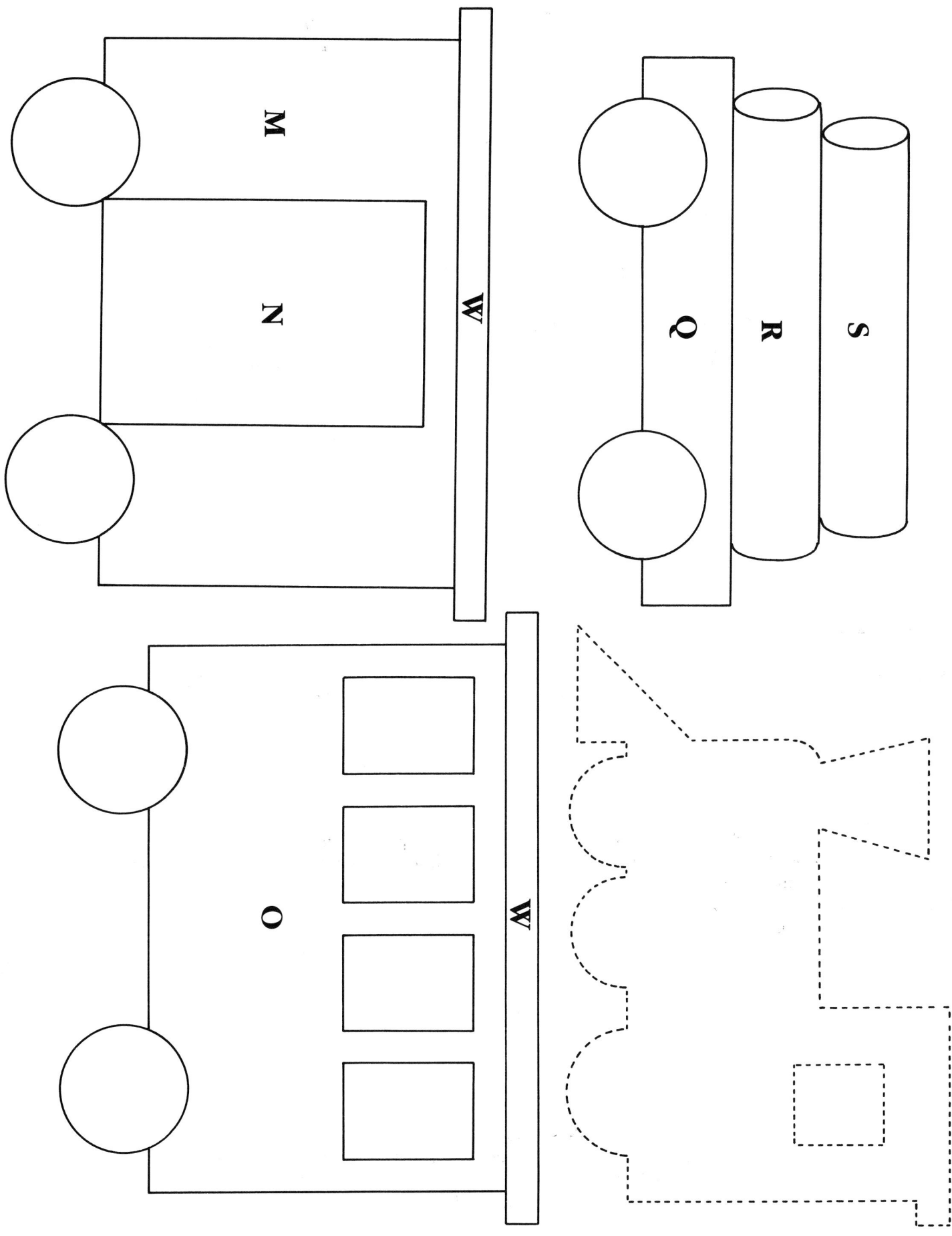

About the Authors

Deborah Gordon's love of fabric, color and pattern led her to a career in commercial interior design, followed by years of teaching needlework, patchwork and quilting. Starting in the 1970's, she has taught for the community college system in Southern California. Deborah estimates that she has taught thousands of students the basics of making quilts.

Specializing in traditional designs, Deborah brings new life to old patterns with different arrangements and inventive color and fabric choices. Her interest in history and a fascination for pattern names led to her first book, *Patches of Glory: An Americana Sampler*, in which she tells the story of many traditional quilt blocks. Deborah lives in Orange, California, with her husband and two sons.

Helen Frost is a familiar name to quilters. Beginning under her maiden name of Young, she coauthored, with Blanche Young, some of the landmark books of the current quilt revival. These featured new construction methods for traditional quilt patterns. Helen is also the coauthor, with Pam Knight Stevenson, of *Grand Endeavors: Vintage Arizona Quilts and Their Makers*. She has taught at guilds and conferences throughout the country and in Europe.

A collector of antique quilts, Helen also prefers traditional patterns for the quilts she makes. Although she is known for her quick machine piecing techniques, her first love is appliqué. She lives in Tucson, Arizona, with her husband, son, and three daughters.

First Star publications:
Nine Patch Wonders by Blanche Young and Helen Young Frost
Patches of Glory: An Americana Sampler by Deborah Gordon
Country Lanes by Blanche Young
Whig Rose Star by Helen Frost